Queer Joy
A Mosaic of Self-Love, Community, and Resistance

Bethany Meier-Evans

Copyright © 2025 by Bethany Meier-Evans

All rights reserved.

No part of this book may be reproduced in any form or by any electronic or mechanical means, including information storage and retrieval systems, without written permission from the author, except for the use of brief quotations in a book review.

Tehom Center Publishing is a 501(c)3 nonprofit publishing feminist and queer authors, with a commitment to elevate BIPOC writers.

Paperback ISBN: 978-1-966655-72-5

Ebook ISBN: 978-1-966655-73-2

Contents

Dedication	5
Acknowledgements	7
A Few Notes as We Begin…	9
Introduction	11

Section 1
What is Queer Joy?

1. Minority Stress	23
2. What is Queer Joy, Anyway?	27
3. Toxic Positivity	31
The Mosaic of Queer Joy	33

Section 2
Loving Yourself

4. Learning to Love Yourself	39
5. Coming Out Stories	43
6. Self-Esteem, Self-Compassion, and Self-Acceptance	49
Mosaic Tile One	53
7. How to Love Yourself	55
8. The Self-Love Toolkit	61
Mosaic Tile Two	67

Section 3
Finding Community

9. Finding Support	73
10. Family of Origin	75
11. Chosen Family	81
12. The Larger Queer Community	87
Mosaic Tile Three	91
13. Virtual Events, Online Support, and Pop Culture	93
14. The Relational Toolkit	97
Mosaic Tile Four	101

Section 4
Rooting Yourself in Liberation

15. Community Action	107
16. Queer Activism and Advocacy	111
Mosaic Tile Five	115
17. Mutual Aid	117
18. The Community Action Toolkit	121
Mosaic Tile Six	127
Assembling Your Mosaic	129
Conclusion	131

Dedication

To my wife, Kelsee, my greatest source of joy: this book wouldn't exist without your love, laughter, and the countless hours you gave me to write. Thank you for lending your creativity to the cover design, for being my sounding board through every brainstorm and revision, and for supporting me through both the good times and the hard ones. Thank you for being my partner, my co-parent, and my best friend. You are my favorite person.

To my son, Ollie: you are the light of my life and the one who taught me what joy truly is. I will always treasure the moments you snuggled with me on the couch while I spent hours on research, the breaks we took to play together, and the way your giggle reminded me why I was writing. This book is for you, and for every child with queer parents—may it help create a brighter, kinder world for families like ours. I love you with every fiber of my being.

Thank you to my mom, Keasha. You were the first to teach me about love and family, the first to help me experience joy, and the first person I came out to. Thank you, too, for being the first to read this book in its entirety, for editing it with care, and for your unwavering support.

To my family, whose love made this book possible; to my chosen family, who laughed, dreamed, and cheered me on; and to my community, who showed up with encouragement, patience, and mutual aid—thank you for being my people.

Thank you to the queer pioneers who showed us that joy can be both resistance and celebration, teaching generations to dance, sing, and fight for our rights without ever losing the joy that has always been our greatest act of defiance. Thank you to the queer community of today, whose courage, laughter, and creativity remind us to live boldly and carry the fight for justice with open and joy-filled hearts. And to our future queer family, may you inherit this joy, this courage, and a community that celebrates every part of who you are.

This book may carry my name on the cover, but it belongs to all of us.

Thank you from the bottom of my heart,
Bethany

Acknowledgements

To the folks who contributed to the GoFundMe—Sid and Katherine Atkin, Brian Nienhouse, Kate Evans, Paula Evans, Diane Baker, and Bethel United Church of Christ in Waterford, MI—you didn't just fund a book, you embodied the spirit of community and mutual aid that this book is about. Thank you for believing in me.

To Naphtali, my writing buddy: thank you for our Wednesday evening co-writing sessions, for encouraging me when my Joy Thief got too loud, for celebrating every small win, and for being a listening ear when I needed it most.

To Angela Yarber and Tehom Center Publishing, thank you for your support, your hard work, and your dedication to lifting up the voices of all of us on the margins.

Thank you to my writing partner, Katie, my beta readers, my launch team, and to everyone else who helped to bring this little book into the world. I will be forever grateful.

A Few Notes as We Begin...

A Note About Triggers:

Queer joy does not exist in a bubble. In this book, we will be celebrating what brings us joy, but we cannot do that without also acknowledging the hardships that our community faces. There will be talk about mental health, hate crimes, bullying, and other potentially triggering topics.

While this is not intended to be a religious book, many of my stories come out of my experiences advocating for the queer community in Christian spaces. At times, I will describe religious trauma and abuse, as well as the ways in which I, my friends, and my clients have moved beyond that trauma.

If you find this material triggering, it is always okay to skip ahead to the next section or set the book down and come back to it later.

A Note About Stories:

The examples in this book have been anonymized to protect the identities of my friends, family, and clients. Certain stories have been altered, or multiple client stories have been combined for clarity. While some details have been adjusted, each story remains a true example of the queer experience.

A Note About the Word Queer:

The word queer has a long history that began in the 15th century, when it was used as an adjective that described something as odd or strange. Over time, society started to use *queer* as a slur against the LGBTQ+ community. This harmful usage of the word queer has been a source of pain for many people who have experienced homophobic and transphobic hatred and bullying. However, language continues to evolve as society evolves. By the 1990s, activists, allies, and scholars within the LGBTQ+ community began to reclaim the word, turning it from a weapon used against us into a symbol of our strength and our defiance.

Today, many people use *queer* as an inclusive and fluid term that reflects the full diversity of our community. It embraces everyone who exists beyond heterosexual and cisgender norms and is often used as a unifying word that holds the expansiveness of the LGBTQ+ spectrum. This is especially important for the identities that can be overlooked or left out, like folks on the asexual (ace) spectrum, people who identify as Two-Spirit, and people who are non-binary and genderfluid.

While I acknowledge that there are some who still find this word painful or choose not to use it, I personally choose to identify as queer because it feels most authentic to my own experience. I also chose to use it throughout this book because I believe it honors the full spectrum of our identities and experiences.

When I write "queer," I mean each and every beautiful, creative, joy-filled person who makes our community whole.

Introduction

On June 27, 2015, my sister and I drove an hour west to Topeka, Kansas. Same-sex marriage had just been legalized across the United States, and we were ready to celebrate. When most people think of places to celebrate a historic achievement for queer rights, I doubt that Topeka is on the top of their lists... but we had a specific, rainbow-painted destination in mind. We were headed to the Equality House.

The brightly colored house sits on an unassuming street in an unassuming neighborhood. It would seem out of place if it weren't intentionally placed directly across from the headquarters of the notorious hate group, Westboro Baptist Church. Its members have made a name for themselves by traveling across America protesting events while holding signs boasting messages like "God Hates Fags" and "Thank God for Dead Soldiers."

In 2013, the organization Planting Peace bought the house across the street and painted it the colors of the Pride flag, transforming it into a symbol of hope for the LGBTQ+ community. I couldn't think of a more fitting place to visit to celebrate our country finally recognizing same-sex marriages.

As we pulled up in front of the rainbow house, my mind raced with memories of the queer advocacy I had been doing since my teenage years. I had worked for so long to help move my community towards acceptance of LGBTQ+ folks, yet I wasn't sure I would ever see the day where marriage equality would be legalized across America. This victory felt so surreal! I kept reading and re-reading the headline of that morning's issue of the *Kansas City Star* as I clutched it tightly in my lap. It proclaimed, in big block letters, that marriage equality was now the "LAW OF THE LAND."

My sister and I jubilantly posed in front of the rainbow house, snapping photos of ourselves holding the newspaper and each other. My eyes welled up as I realized that this was one of the best moments of my life. And yet, through those joyful tears, I couldn't help but take in the fenced-off "church" across the street. The cream-colored building, with tall fencing and several security cameras, displayed a white banner with red letters that declared, "God Hates America." The marquee near the front gate read: "Gay Marriage Dooms Nations." In that instant, I was reminded that while we had reached an important milestone, the fight for true equality was far from over.

I think this is how many queer folks feel on a daily basis. Our identities, our communities, and our stories are full of joy, but hatred and bigotry still show up in our neighborhoods, our workplaces, and our families. It can be hard to focus on joy when it feels like so much of the world is against us.

As I write this, in the United States of America in 2025, almost every day brings new executive orders aimed at erasing us and amplifying hate against us. When so many in our community are simply struggling to survive, it can feel almost irresponsible to talk about joy. But that's exactly why queer joy matters.

This book is an exploration of joy. Together, we will discover how we choose it, nurture it, and let it sustain us. Joy is a necessary part of our fight for justice. It is the fuel that helps us keep moving forward. Now is the time for each of us to claim it, every single day and in every space we inhabit!

The prevailing narrative in our society is that the queer experience is one of pain and suffering. I disagree. Queer joy is not only attainable but *transformative*—because it grows from loving yourself, from finding a community that loves you for who you are, and from rooting yourself in liberation.

Audre Lorde, black, lesbian, feminist, and poet, once wrote, "There is no such thing as a single-issue struggle because we do not live single-issue lives.[1]" In that same spirit, I believe we cannot heal from the burdens of homophobia, transphobia, and bigotry through a single path. Healing requires a holistic and multi-faceted approach. To truly live joy-filled lives, we must learn to love ourselves, find and build community, and commit to making the world a kinder, more joyful place for all.

When we love ourselves, we embrace our whole being with compassion and acceptance. This love must be the foundation of queer joy, because it nurtures resilience and empowers us to live authentically, in spite of external challenges.

Being loved for who we are means receiving acceptance and affirmation from others who honor our true selves. This love builds community and belonging, reminding us that we are not alone and that our identity is worthy of celebration.

Rooting ourselves in liberation means grounding our lives in freedom from oppressive norms and embracing the power to define our own identity and path. It is essential, because it transforms joy from a fleeting feeling into a radical, enduring act of resistance and self-determination. And it is expansive.

As an Interfaith Minister of Queer Joy & Creative Liberation, I help LGBTQ+ folks and their communities cultivate joy, spirit, and justice through art, ritual, and sacred storytelling. I am a writer, speaker, and the host of the *Joyfully Queer Podcast*. I am also a Reiki master, an ordained minister in the Christian tradition, and a first-degree Wiccan Priestess in the tradition of Stone Circle Wicca. I offer one-on-one coaching, spiritual direction through Tarot and Reiki, as well as workshops, classes, and resources for building joyful and affirming communities. My passion is helping people find and experience queer joy—in their own lives and their communities.

But, I haven't always embraced joy.

In the summer of 2022, after nearly 20 years of advocacy for the LGBTQ+ community, I burned out.

I burned out hard.

The truth is, I had been stretching myself too thin for years. I pushed myself through an undergraduate degree and two master's

---

1. Lorde, Audre. *Sister Outsider: Essays and Speeches.* Trumansburg, NY: Crossing Press, 1984, 144.

degrees while working full-time. I pushed myself through a six-month, cross-country bus ride, where I advocated for queer students in Christian universities and other spaces. I pushed myself through internships and certificate courses, an intensive ordination process into the United Church of Christ, and years of training to become a Reiki master. I did all of this while remaining committed to activism and advocacy for the LGBTQ+ community everywhere I could.

As someone devoted to a life of service, I was constantly putting other people first and ignoring my own needs. That's what those of us in "helping professions" are supposed to do, right?

In 2020, my wife and I moved across the country to New Mexico, where I had just accepted a position as minister of a queer-affirming congregation. I was trying to preach compelling, justice-oriented sermons each week and hold an aging congregation together through a global pandemic... while at the same time receiving hate mail and nasty phone calls from people in the broader community telling me that I was a sinner who was leading people straight to hell.

And then I started waking up in the morning more tired than when I had gone to bed. I was having panic attacks in the pulpit. I ended up on three different antidepressant/anti-anxiety medications. I had literally pushed my body, mind, and spirit so hard that they staged a protest, and I had no choice but to listen. Finally, after years of pouring my time and energy into others, I chose to focus on my own healing.

That choice wasn't easy. It meant walking away from the profession that I had spent over a decade working towards. It meant confronting my own insecurities, while feeling as though I had disappointed the people and systems that had supported me through my work. And it meant becoming less financially stable as my wife and I went from a two-income household to a one-income household.

The year that followed wasn't easy either, but it was crucial to my development into the person I am today. I found healing in the things that I loved– like working with animals and starting a small art business with my wife. Petsitting, dog-walking, and selling art didn't cover most of our bills, but they helped keep us afloat while I did the deeper work of healing, growing, and discovering who I truly am.

I realized that while I have been working toward equality and justice for my community, I hadn't been doing it with joy. Twenty years after I came out, the prevailing messaging in our society is still that being born queer is a hardship. When we come out, we risk losing friends, family, and spiritual communities. Too many of us become victims of hate crimes. We face discrimination in our workplaces, educational institutions, and housing. Our youth are bullied in schools, and that continues to worsen as legislation seeks to prohibit trans students from socially transitioning.

These are all real and true issues that affect us, and there is nothing wrong with talking about them. In fact, we must bring attention to the things that bring us pain and attempt to silence us. However, I have learned that focusing only on the negative aspects of being queer does us a disservice. I spent years lifting up the painful experiences of being queer to implore the people in my community to become LGBTQ+ allies, but doing so took a toll on my mental health. Not because what I was saying wasn't true, but because it wasn't the whole story.

Queer joy is a radical act. It exists in defiance of a world that too often tells us that our existence is one of tragedy. Yes, injustice is real. Discrimination is real. The weight of systemic oppression is real. But so is the laughter of a group of queer friends dancing at a beachside resort, their bodies moving with unrestrained freedom. So is the warmth of holding your partner's hand without fear, the quiet intimacy of love free of shame. And so is the pride of being fully, unapologetically yourself, of choosing authenticity over conformity.

After my wife and I bought our house in the New Mexican desert, we started turning that house into a home. One of the first ways we did this was through planting a garden in our backyard, along with various trees and bushes around our property. For two Midwesterners, gardening in the desert brought a lot of new challenges. No matter how much water and shade we tried to supply, plants we thought would take root and blossom were scorched by the desert sun. The dry dirt was not welcoming to everything we planted; we watched beautiful trees, bushes, and plants die because they could not find what they needed to flourish.

It would be easy for people to point out our failures when we share about our efforts at homesteading: the $80 orange tree that died too quickly, the blueberry bushes that shriveled once we put them into the ground, and the carrots and tomatoes that never sprouted. But focusing on that would do our little homestead a disservice. All of that is true, but it would ignore the five lavender plants that blossom along our walkway, providing life to the many pollinators in our yard. It would ignore the beautiful sunflowers that grow as tall as me. It would ignore the plethora of zucchini that we were able to freeze and use over the winter. Most importantly, focusing on our failures would have taken the joy out of gardening, perhaps even causing us to give up on homesteading altogether.

In a similar way, I have realized that, as queer people, we simply cannot expect to be happy, healthy, and whole while only focusing on the parts of our lives that are painful. Our authentic expression—of love, of joy, of celebration—is a gift to the world. It sustains us. It makes us whole. My passion for queer justice and equality shifted with that realization. I decided that, just as I had found joy in my garden, I also wanted to cultivate the joy that makes being queer worth celebrating.

Queer joy is not about ignoring reality. It is about *defiance*. It is refusing to let oppression be the only story told about our community and our lives. Queer joy is about writing our own narratives. If we talk only about our pain, we allow ourselves to be defined by that pain. But the queer experience is about *so much more* than just suffering. It is full of love, community, laughter, and resilience. Joy is what has kept our community alive through generations of injustice, and it is what will continue to keep us moving forward. Queer people *deserve* happiness. We deserve joy *right now*, we cannot wait for everything to be perfect.

In a world where many don't want us to exist, queer joy is a lifeline. It is what sustains us in the midst of our struggles, what connects us to one another, and what gives us hope for a better tomorrow.

I need queer joy now more than ever. And, since you are reading this book, you may need it too. I invite you to join me as we explore what queer joy is, why it matters, and how we can find it through loving ourselves, finding our community, and working towards creating a more joyful world. Throughout this book, you will encounter true stories of queer joy and transformation, accessible research from experts across a variety of disciplines, and easy-to-follow guidelines for finding joy in your own life. There are also exercises, journal prompts, and reflection activities to help you discover and celebrate the queer joy in your own life.

In **Section One**, we will discuss minority stress, the value of queer joy, and the differences between joy, happiness, and toxic positivity.

In **Section Two**, we will explore the importance of creating your own joy and the steps to do so through accepting and celebrating your own identity.

In **Section Three**, we will focus on how we can find joy through the people we surround ourselves with, including local and online queer communities, as well as affirming friends, family, and spaces.

And in **Section Four**, we will learn how we can do our part to help spread joy by making our communities more welcoming for LGBTQ+ folks through activism, advocacy, and mutual aid.

Queer joy begins within, as you dare to discover how to love yourself fully, fiercely, and without apology. It grows as you find your people– the ones who see you, celebrate you, and hold space for your becoming. It takes root in the world as you rise to advocate, not just for your own liberation, but for the joy and dignity of every queer soul still fighting to be free.

You are being called forward. It is time to claim your worth, to gather your community, and to live in ways that shift the world toward justice—and joy! Finding and harnessing the power of queer joy in my own life has been a game-changer, and I can't wait to share this journey with you.

Turn the page. Let's begin!

Questions for Reflection:

- What does the phrase "queer joy" mean to me?
- What are my biggest hopes for what I will gain from this book?

Section 1

What is Queer Joy?

"If you can't love yourself, how in the hell are you gonna love somebody else?"

— RuPaul

"Because I... I don't want to look ugly..." I said, feeling the weight of the honest vulnerability that came with that statement.

My wife gaped at me as I shifted my eyes to the floor in shame.

"What?!" she said. "Babe, you're not ugly!! It doesn't matter what haircut you get, you're going to look great. And if you don't like it, it's just hair, it will grow back."

I nodded slowly, sighed, and rose from our brown leather sofa to escape the conversation.

"Why would you think that you'd look ugly?" she asked, peering up at me.

I shrugged noncommittally and brushed it off, saying, "Yeah, you're right. If I don't like it, it will just grow back." I gathered up the baby bottles that sat on the coffee table and made my way into the kitchen to wash them.

As I filled our sink with soapy water, my mind wandered again to the haircut I was planning to get. For days, I had been asking my wife's opinion on whether I would look good with a haircut that was much shorter than I usually wear. I had been playing with the idea of getting a fauxhawk-style haircut that would be cool during the summer in the desert. Our son had just reached the age where he was pulling on everything he could wrap his tiny fingers around, and it seemed like now would be a great time to just chop all the extra hair off. Every time I felt close to making the decision to do it, though, I became anxious.

This wasn't like me. I have always expressed myself through my hair, which means that its style has been constantly evolving and changing. I've grown it out well past my shoulders and then cut it into a short pixie cut. I've had it wavy, and it's been straight. I've had the sides shaved and an undercut. I've colored it every color under the sun, most frequently a combination of pink, purple, and blue. I am not someone who is normally particular about my hair, so it's no wonder my wife was perplexed by my overthinking this one cut.

My mind wandered as I washed bottle after bottle, swirling the brush inside each one to clean any residue of formula that might be left. As I dunked my arms into the warm suds, it struck me—maybe I wasn't worried about being ugly. Maybe what I was worried about was being perceived as queer.

But I love being queer. I love my wife, I love my chosen family, I love my community. I love rainbows and drag queens and that feeling of belonging that I get at Pride festivals. I've been out of the closet since I was a teenager. I'm literally writing a book about how being queer brings me joy… how could I possibly be struggling with anxiety about being more visibly queer? Why, after being a queer activist for over 20 years, was I fighting internalized homophobia?

And then I thought about the boy who called me a "bull dyke" as he passed me in the hallway after I started our high school's Gay-Straight Alliance. I remembered the way he met up with his buddy at the lockers and loudly said, "Dykes are just girls who are too ugly to get a man, so they try to become one instead."

And I thought about my first college roommate who refused to move into our dorm room when she found out on Facebook that I was queer.

And I thought about the time that I squeezed behind the locked door of a small motel room with 17 other LGBTQ+ people in Nashville, hiding from the men who were spitting at us and spewing derogatory names just for "being queer" in their presence.

And I thought about how, in many ways, the world feels more dangerous today than it did back then. Suddenly, the internalized homophobia I was feeling made a little more sense.

Standing there in the kitchen, I felt the weight of it all—the fear, the risks, the buried doubts. This was followed by the thought of how long I'd been standing up to prejudice, discrimination, and hatred. When I was being bullied in high school, I didn't shrink back. Instead, I started a club that was a welcoming place for myself and other queer kids and allies in the school. When my roommate refused to move in with me, I made new friends in the dorm. After we called the police on the men who were harassing us in Nashville, I pulled myself together, and then I attended an event where I advocated for queer students at a Christian college that had discriminatory policies against the LGBTQ+ community.

I didn't back down in any of those situations, so I certainly wasn't going to let myself be intimidated by a haircut. I took my hands out of the soapy sink, wiped them on the dish towel, and pulled out my phone. It was time to make an appointment.

Minority Stress

To understand queer joy, we have to begin with some context. Our joy exists in the real world, where queer folks carry the invisible weight of knowing that our society wasn't built with us in mind. In this chapter we will be focusing on the relentless, cumulative weight of discrimination, hypervigilance, and internalized shame that comes from living in a society where queerness is often marginalized or erased.

Everyone experiences some level of stress in their day-to-day lives; it is simply a part of the human experience. For example, most people feel stressed about starting a new job. However, heterosexual and cisgender people generally don't need to worry about being fired or discriminated against for coming out at their workplace.

The concept that queer folks experience unique stressors because of our identities is called **Minority Stress**—the stress that a marginalized person experiences because they are living in an environment that was created for the majority.[1]

Alongside running my own business, I make extra money by pet sitting. Multiple times a month, I enter the homes of new clients and meet them and their families for the first time. Many pet sitters may

---

1. Frost, D. M., and I. H. Meyer. "Minority Stress Theory: Application, Critique, and Continued Relevance." *Current Opinion in Psychology* 51 (June 2023): 101579. https://doi.org/10.1016/j.copsyc.2023.101579.

feel a little nervous about meeting a new client; however, I carry a specific set of concerns that most others do not need to worry about.

When I enter someone's home, I look around at their décor, trying to gauge if it's safe for me to be out to them. I wonder: *Can they tell I am queer from my haircut and the way I dress? Should I mention my wife, or should I say "spouse" or "partner" instead? Am I safe in this house, with these new people, or will they figure out that I'm queer and say or do something harmful toward me?* These questions are not unique to me, queer people around the world ask similar questions every single day.

When faced with these challenges, it's no wonder that queer and trans people experience higher rates of anxiety, depression, and PTSD. The LGBTQ+ community is often faced with discrimination, internalized shame, social exclusion, and the pressure to hide or suppress our identities, all of which are a burden on our mental health.

This experience is often compounded by intersecting marginalized identities. Female-identified queer people experience both homophobia and sexism. Queer people of color experience racism along with homophobia and/or transphobia. Classism, ableism, fatphobia, and other forms of discrimination can intersect with homophobia and transphobia to cause even more stress, anxiety, and mental health difficulties.

Despite these challenges, joy creates space for affirmation, connection, and hope. When queer people are open to experiencing joy, it helps us cope with trauma and celebrate our identity and self-worth. In turn, celebrating who we are can help us become more resilient and even heal from the harm we have experienced.

When we talk about queer joy, I believe we are talking about a mental health resource that is as vital as therapy. While it does not take the place of therapy (and I am not a therapist), I believe that joy is essential because it gives us the strength to keep moving forward. It's joy that helps us resist the prejudice and discriminatory policies that make our lives harder. It's joy that makes our authentic lives worth fighting for. However, our joy exists in tension with a world that often tries to silence or erase it. Internalized queerphobia, discrimination, stigma, and institutional oppression are real, ongoing forces that block access to joy and well-being.

Some Barriers to Queer Joy:

- **Internalized Queerphobia/Homophobia/Transphobia** refers to the negative feelings and beliefs that queer people have about their own identity. This stems from growing up in a world full of negative attitudes toward queer people. Even when we know that these feelings are unfair and biased, it can be hard for us to unlearn them.
- **Discrimination** is unjust or prejudicial treatment against a specific group of people. For queer folks, discrimination can take many forms. It can range from subtle microaggressions—like ignorant and hurtful comments—to being denied housing, harassed on the street, or fired from a job.
- **Stigma** is created by negative and harmful beliefs about a group of people. It convinces us that our identities are something to be ashamed of, something to be hidden or merely tolerated. Stigma tells queer people that our full selves are too much, that our joy is inappropriate, or that our love is less legitimate than heterosexual love.
- **Institutional oppression** happens when discrimination and stigma become legalized through the government, our workplaces, school systems, and other institutions. From bans on same-sex marriage to barring trans kids from playing sports, institutional oppression gives prejudice and discrimination the power to harm us.

Despite all of this, queer people continue to find ways to create joy. Even in the face of discrimination, stigma, and oppression, we continue to build community, celebrate love, share laughter, and make art that reflects our truth. We fight for this joy because we know that it matters.

What is Queer Joy, Anyway?

For the purposes of this book, I describe queer joy as the feeling we get when our identity and our true, unrestricted selves align with our experiences. This definition of joy comes from Jeffrey J. Arnett's article, "Joy: An Integrative Theory," in the *Journal of Positive Psychology:*

> This paper proposes a new theory of joy as defined by *the elation of right relation,* i.e., an intense and temporary feeling of heightened positive emotion as a consequence of a *just right* fit between our identity and the moment we are experiencing…
>
> In the state of joy, there is a match between our identity and what we are experiencing. "This is great. Life is *good*. This could hardly be better." It can last moments, minutes, even hours, but it is not perpetual. Nevertheless, people vary in their readiness for joy, and their opportunities for it, and consequently in the frequency of their joyful experiences.[1]

Queer joy is the positive feeling that comes from the deep, affirming, and sometimes even rebellious experience of being authentically you. It can be found in the laughter shared between chosen family, the

---

1. Arnett, J. J. "Joy: An Integrative Theory." *The Journal of Positive Psychology* 18, no. 1 (2022): 1–14. https://doi.org/10.1080/17439760.2022.2053878.

feeling of being truly seen and loved for who you are, and the sense of belonging in spaces that are fully welcoming and supportive of your identity.

I find queer joy in the smile lines of my wife's face. I experience it in the thrill of getting a new haircut or an outfit that helps me feel more comfortable in my own skin. I feel it in the pediatrician's office when our son's doctor refers to both my wife and me as his parents. It was powerfully present in the exhilaration I felt while belting out "The Story" with other queer fans at a Brandi Carlile concert. Anything that makes you feel fully alive in your queerness is queer joy.

While joy and happiness are often used interchangeably, they can mean very different things. For the purposes of this book:

- **Happiness** is often tied to external circumstances—it is a reaction to positive events, a fleeting state influenced by someone's environment.
    - *Example: Going on vacation makes me happy.*
- **Joy**, on the other hand, is deeper and tied to your internal being. It is not dependent on external validation or ideal conditions, and it can exist even in difficult times because it is rooted in authenticity, meaning, and connection.
    - *Example: Standing with my community at a Pride event fills me with queer joy.*

On the surface, joy and happiness can feel like two similar experiences; however, distinguishing between the two is important when we look at the challenges faced by the LGBTQ+ community. While happiness comes from good things happening *to* us, queer joy is an internal experience that persists *despite* and *through* difficult times.

For queer folks, joy is particularly powerful because it lives inside each one of us. It emerges from within, regardless of our circumstances. It comes from embracing our identities, celebrating our unique self-expressions, and forming communities that affirm and uplift us. It can even be a form of resistance against the societal norms and laws that marginalize our queer identities.

In *"Queer Joy as Rage: A Tool to Transform,"* E. Jeremy Torres explains:

Queer joy transcends mere contentment with one's existence; it encompasses optimism as a force propelling the movement toward equity. When marginalized identities become politicized, maintaining moments of genuine love and radical activism becomes a delicate balance. Preserving queer joy becomes not only essential for personal well-being but a means to center survival and resistance... The power of queer joy extends beyond personal experience—it becomes a formidable weapon against unjust systems. Thus, queer joy emerges as a radical tool against heterosexist and heterogendered systems of oppression.[2]

By embracing queer joy, we can find strength, resilience, and a sense of empowerment that is more enduring than temporary happiness.

---

2. Torres, E. "Queer Joy as Rage: A Tool to Transform." *The Vermont Connection* 45, no. 1 (2024). https://scholarworks.uvm.edu/tvc/vol45/iss1/2.

Toxic Positivity

In today's political climate, where anti-LGBTQ+ legislation, book bans, and attacks on trans rights are on the rise, the concept of queer joy holds profound significance. Yet, it is important to distinguish queer joy from toxic positivity, which dismisses real struggles in favor of forced optimism. Toxic positivity insists on happiness no matter the circumstances, silencing our true experiences.

According to Dr. Zoe Wyatt in the article, *The Dark Side of #PositiveVibes: Understanding Toxic Positivity in Modern Culture*, "Toxic positivity, while rooted in well-meaning intentions, can lead to significant psychological harm when it dismisses or invalidates genuine emotional experiences.[1]"

This mindset can be particularly harmful to queer individuals, who are often told to "focus on progress" or "just be themselves" without acknowledging the systemic barriers and real dangers that our community faces. Queer joy is not about ignoring these hardships. Rather, it is about creating moments of celebration *despite* them. It is about finding community, love, and affirmation even in the face of adversity. This is where it differs from toxic positivity, which dismisses

---

1. Wyatt, Zoe. "The Dark Side of #PositiveVibes: Understanding Toxic Positivity in Modern Culture." *Psychiatry and Behavioral Health* 3 (2024): 1–6. https://doi.org/10.33425/2833-5449.0016.

or invalidates pain with messages like "just be happy" or "look on the bright side."

- **Toxic positivity** forces people to suppress or deny negative emotions, creating a false sense of well-being.
- **Queer joy** acknowledges struggle while refusing to let oppression define the entire queer experience. It is about finding light in the darkness, not pretending the darkness does not exist.

Queer joy allows space for grief, anger, and resistance while also making room for love, celebration, and playfulness. It is a declaration that we, as queer people, deserve to thrive, not merely survive.

In 2012, the owner of Chick-fil-A garnered national attention when he said that his company believes in the "Biblical definition of a family" and does not support same-sex marriage. In response, queer activists held a nationwide "Kiss-In" at Chick-fil-A locations. They arrived in droves, carrying signs that read, "We're Here, We're Queer, and We're Not Eating Here!" and "Love Makes a Family!" Queer couples kissed, held hands, and sang in front of the restaurants. While they were protesting something painful and discriminatory, these activists created joy with chants that turned into dancing.

Unlike toxic positivity, which demands suppression of negative emotions, queer joy makes space for them, recognizing that challenging feelings can exist alongside joy rather than in opposition to it. When fear and uncertainty loom large for LGBTQ+ people, joy becomes an act of defiance. By embracing queer joy, we refuse to let oppression steal our ability to celebrate and connect with one another. Our joy is a reminder that no matter what laws are passed or what lies are spread about us, queer people will continue to find ways to build a future rooted in community, resilience, and hope.

Questions for Reflection:

- How can I feel joy amidst challenging circumstances?
- How have I been harmed by toxic positivity?
- How do I currently define joy, and has that definition changed over time?

The Mosaic of Queer Joy

Now that you know what queer joy *is,* you can begin to discover how to invite it into your life. Think of this next stage as a journey that blends reflection with creativity and invites your whole self into the process.

Throughout the remainder of this book, you'll find gentle invitations to pause, to listen inward, and to express yourself. Each reflection will guide you to design a single tile that corresponds to a color in the original Pride flag. Once completed, you will have six tiles that come together to form your personal Mosaic of Queer Joy.

Art has a way of speaking what words cannot.

We carry deep truths in our queer bodies—truths about who we are and what brings us joy. Sometimes, that joy is meant to be experienced rather than explained. Often, we can explore these truths more easily through our creative expressions.

This is your opportunity to play, get messy, and experiment! This is *your* mosaic, an exploration of *your* joy. No one is grading you or judging you on your artistic ability. As you can see from the examples throughout the book, the goal is to enjoy the process, not stress about the end result!

Each mosaic page offers an opportunity for you to color, paint, draw, collage, or write. There is no right or wrong way to do this!

Each tile you make will be connected with a core theme: self-love, community, or liberation/activism. You'll reflect on the questions provided and respond through a creative practice of your choice. As you do so, you may begin to notice what joy feels like as you shape it yourself.

By the end of this book, you'll have created six small tiles. When placed together, they will form a mosaic: a visual remembrance of your queer joy. Remember, this is not about creating a perfect image. Rather, it is an opportunity to embrace your healing journey and celebrate your joy in a new way!

Section 2

Loving Yourself

"Owning our story and loving ourselves through that process is the bravest thing we'll ever do."

— Brené Brown, *The Gifts of Imperfection*

It was a cold, snowy morning in the Wasatch Mountain Range in northern Utah. I sat in the stillness of a darkened room, watching the snow fall against the frosted window. Outside, it blanketed the pine branches and piled on the ground around the retreat center. The snow was so deep that the three vanloads of women who had arrived the night before were encouraged to wear snowshoes if they chose to venture out.

I had come here to mend. I wasn't entirely sure what that would mean, only that something in me felt cracked. Not shattered, not ruined, just... fragile.

I held the morning schedule in my hands and sighed. The first session of the retreat for trauma survivors was simply labeled, "Opening: Art Workshop." I was sure it would be some silly collage-making class, or that we would be sketching our emotions using crayons and markers. I had previously heard there was merit to art therapy, but I was here to do real work.

"Trust the process," I mumbled to myself as I grabbed my bag and a sweater and headed to the art room.

I smiled at one of my roommates as I slid into the chair next to her.

"Any idea what we are doing this morning?" she asked, as we both pulled out the purple folders we'd received at orientation.

"No clue," I replied. "Probably something to ease us into the day. I'm looking forward to the meditation and mindfulness workshop after this, though!"

The room quieted as one of the therapists started the class by inviting each of us to go to a cabinet in the corner and pick out a piece of pottery that "spoke to us." The shelves were full of a variety of colorful bowls and cups, saucers and small vases. I picked up a beautiful ivory bowl decorated with delicate pink flowers and headed back to my seat.

"Before we begin today, I want to invite you to take a deep breath with me. Inhale... and exhale," the therapist said. "You're here. You're safe. You're not alone."

"Today, we're going to work with a beautiful and symbolic Japanese art form called *Kintsugi*. In kintsugi, broken pottery is repaired with a special lacquer mixed with powdered gold. Instead of hiding the cracks, the artist highlights them—making them part of the piece's story. The broken places don't make the bowl useless; they make it more beautiful, more unique, and more resilient.

I want to be really clear about something: this is not about glorifying pain or saying that trauma is beautiful. It's about honoring your healing. It's about saying, *Yes, I've been broken. And I'm still here. And now, I get to decide how I put myself back together.*

Each of you has a ceramic bowl or cup in front of you. You can choose to break it yourself, or I can help you do that when you're ready. Once it's broken, we'll take time to sit with the pieces. Just notice how they feel. You might feel emotions come up—grief, anger, pride, even numbness. All of that is welcome here."

I held the small bowl in my hands, running my finger along its intricate design. As the women around me began taking turns with a hammer, I was struck by how deeply saddened I was. The room around me was full of the sounds of things breaking, but I suddenly felt desperate to keep my bowl safe. I clutched it to my chest as my eyes welled up with tears. This bowl was beautiful; it didn't deserve to be broken.

"Trust the process," I whispered to myself. I gently wrapped the bowl in a towel, laid it down on the floor, and waited for my turn with the hammer.

At first, I hit the bowl much too softly. The hammer came down, and nothing happened. I felt my breath catch in my chest as I struck it once more, harder this time.

I passed the hammer to my roommate and slowly unwrapped the towel that was still holding the broken fragments of the bowl together. Inside were three large ceramic pieces and two smaller ones. I laid them out in front of me as my mind wandered to the times I, too, had felt broken, to the things that I still needed to heal from.

I stared at the shards of the bowl that moments ago had been perfect, as I pulled my sweatshirt tighter around myself. I wasn't sure if it was because of the cold mountain air or because I needed to feel held, protected from the memories that had left me, also, in shattered pieces.

I wiped away a tear and took another deep breath, bringing myself back to the present moment.

The therapist was directing our group on how to mix the glue and the gold powder together, creating a shimmering adhesive to apply to the jagged edges of our broken pottery. I began spreading the thick, golden paste onto the edges of the bowl.

The process wasn't easy, but healing never is. In the end, I turned the bowl over and over in my hands, tracing the golden lines with my fingers. It would never look the way it once did, but that was the point. It wasn't ruined. It wasn't less. It was still whole. Still beautiful. And maybe... I was, too.

That morning, in the quiet snow-covered mountains, I began to understand something that I hadn't before: healing doesn't erase the pain, it transforms it. And in that transformation, there is beauty, there is strength, and yes... there is joy.

Learning to Love Yourself

Accepting and loving oneself can change everything.

I have never met a queer person who has not been impacted by toxic, homophobic, or transphobic messaging from society. These negative messages tell us that we are wrong for simply being who we are or for loving who we love. This can cause us not only to feel ashamed to admit to ourselves that we are queer, but also to feel afraid to come out to others for fear of rejection.

Here's the truth: You are a person who deserves to take up space and to be loved for who you are.

When we begin to trust that we are worthy of love, we also begin to heal. Loving ourselves for who we are softens the voice of shame in our minds. It teaches us that we are not unlovable, not broken, not too much, and not a mistake. When we heal, we learn to make choices from a place of self-confidence instead of a place of shame. We stop chasing approval and start building lives that actually feel like our own.

And from that healing, queer joy begins to grow.

Decades of research show that queer people "who have accepted and integrated their sexual orientations ultimately have greater psychological well-being than those who have not.[1]" In other words,

---

1. Henry, Meghan Marie. *Coming Out: Implications for Self-Esteem and Depression in Gay*

when we accept ourselves for who we are and live our lives authentically, we are happier, healthier, and more at peace.

You may remember from the previous chapter that my definition of queer joy is "the feeling we get when our identity and our true, unrestricted selves align with our experiences." For this to happen, we must first accept ourselves for being queer.

That may sound easy, but learning how to truly accept and love ourselves is a process. When someone is conditioned throughout their childhood to live their life as a straight, cisgender person, the shock to their system when they realize they are queer can be overwhelming. One may wonder, *What will my life look like now? Will I be happy? Will I find love? Will my family and friends accept me for who I am?*

One of the best ways to reach self-acceptance and authenticity is through the coming out process. In 1979, psychologist Vivienne Cass developed the model, *"Cass Model of Gay and Lesbian Identity Development*[2]*"* after years of studying gay and lesbian individuals. Since then, researchers have been using this model to expand their understanding of coming out and how it affects the queer community.[3]

In recent years, the Cass model has faced several critiques. First, it was developed in the 1970s, and our understanding of sexual orientation and gender identity has grown immensely since then. Second, it was created from research on people who identified as gay or lesbian, and we now know that the queer umbrella is much larger than those two identities. Third, it is a rigid model, and we now know that coming out can be influenced and shaped by many different factors. While some people may follow these stages, others may skip a stage, move through the stages more fluidly, or have a different experience altogether.

Despite all of this, I do believe that Cass's six stages of coming out are a helpful, albeit imperfect, framework for us to understand the process of acknowledging, wrestling with, and ultimately accepting

---

and Lesbian Individuals. California State Polytechnic University, Humboldt, 2013. http://hdl.handle.net/2148/1492.

2. Vivienne C. Cass, "Homosexual Identity Formation: A Theoretical Model," *Journal of Homosexuality* 4, no. 3 (1979): 219–235, https://doi.org/10.1300/J082v04n03_01.

3. Degges-White, S., B. Rice, and J. E. Myers. "Revisiting Cass' Theory of Sexual Identity Formation: A Study of Lesbian Development." *Journal of Mental Health Counseling* 22, no. 4 (2000): 318–333.

our queer identities. Cass's model of homosexual identity formation can be understood through the following adapted framework:

- **Stage One: Identity Confusion**—The person begins to question whether they may be a member of the LGBTQ+ community.
- **Stage Two: Identity Comparison**—The person continues to question if they are queer while also noticing that they feel different or isolated from parts of society.
- **Stage Three: Identity Tolerance**—The person begins seeking out, exploring, and identifying with the LGBTQ+ community.
- **Stage Four: Identity Acceptance**—The person becomes more accepting of their queer identity and starts to come out to important people in their life.
- **Stage Five: Identity Pride**—The person becomes more confident in their queer identity, comes out to the majority of people, and feels proud of being a part of the LGBTQ+ community.
- **Stage Six: Identity Synthesis**—The person has successfully reconciled their identity as queer or trans with who they are as a person[4].

I have taken these six stages and refined them into three categories:

- **Coming Out to Yourself**—The internal recognition and acceptance of your identity.
- **Coming Out to Others**—Sharing your identity with people in your life.
- **Living Authentically as Your Full Self**—Embracing your queerness in daily life, integrating it into all aspects of who you are, and allowing it to shape how you love, connect with others, and move through the world.

Join me in the next chapter as we travel through these three steps with my clients Mandy and Mason.

---

4. Adapted from Cass, "Homosexual Identity Formation: A Theoretical Model,"

Coming Out Stories

Mandy's Story

Coming Out to Yourself

For most of her life, Mandy didn't question her sexuality. She didn't think she needed to. She had crushes on boys, loved romantic stories, and even had a couple of relationships. But there was always something about the way she moved through the world that didn't quite align with what she saw and heard from others.

As a teenager, when her friends would make jokes or comments about sex, she often sat quietly, wondering, *Is that funny? Is that something people actually think about all the time?* It was never something that repulsed her, but it also wasn't something she connected with. Her first kiss, with a boy she really liked, left her confused. It's not that it was bad, it just felt... mechanical. *Where do I put my head? My lips? What am I supposed to feel?* There was no rush of desire, no emotional undercurrent, just the sense that she was doing what people expected.

That quiet difference followed her for years. Occasionally, she joked that maybe she was asexual, but the word never quite fit. It felt too final, too black-and-white. She *had* experienced attraction before, but only rarely, and never in the way other people described. She was waiting for a word that felt... right.

One night, while scrolling through TikTok in bed, Mandy stumbled across a video from a creator talking about the term *demisexual*. She paused. Watched it once. Then again. And again. Something clicked.

That word was the beginning of everything.

She dove into research, reading about the Asexual spectrum, learning its nuances, discovering that attraction could look many different ways. The more she read, the more she saw herself. She realized that her attraction was deeply tied to emotional connection, and that even when it was present, physical intimacy wasn't something that she necessarily craved.

At the same time, she understood that while she was somewhere on the ace spectrum, she wasn't aromantic. In fact, she loved romance. She devoured novels, delighted in Hallmark movies, and even owned a Taylor Swift and Travis Kelce fan sweatshirt. She was *so* romantic. Just… not sexual. At least, not in the typical sense.

Finding the word *demisexual* unlocked a sense of self she didn't realize she was missing. It gave her clarity. But more than that, it gave her *joy*, the quiet, satisfying joy of seeing herself clearly and knowing she wasn't alone.

Coming Out to Others

Coming out to others was less dramatic than Mandy had feared. When she told her mom, her reaction was simple: "Yeah, that makes sense." Her mom even shared a story about how, when Mandy was a baby, she only wanted to be held facing outward. She always wanted closeness, but on her own terms. That had never changed.

She told close friends next, starting with a casual Zoom call where she said, "So… I've been thinking about this, and I think I've found my word." Her friends received it with warmth and respect, letting the moment matter without turning it into a spectacle.

She began sharing more widely—telling her brother, some coworkers, and a few friends in passing. Sometimes she used the word demisexual, sometimes just ace. Not everyone understood right away. One jokingly asked, "So… are you still hetero?" Others were puzzled by the contradiction of loving romance but identifying as asexual. Overall, she was met with curiosity and kindness.

What surprised her most was how good it felt to say the words out loud, to be truly known by the people she loved.

Living Authentically as Your Full Self

For Mandy, the deepest joy came not from the act of coming out, but from the integration that followed. She began to feel whole in a way she hadn't known she was missing. She stopped trying to fit herself into expectations about intimacy, dating, and desire that had never worked for her. She no longer felt broken or behind. She understood her own rhythms now, the slow unfolding of emotional connection, the longing for companionship without the pressure for physical intimacy, and the way her deepest love showed up in friendship, family, and community.

She realized she didn't need to swipe endlessly or go on awkward dates in noisy bars. She didn't need to chase someone else's version of love. What she needed was understanding.

In that understanding, she found contentment. For Mandy, queer joy is the joy of self-awareness. It is the joy of discovering that she isn't broken, that she isn't wrong, and that her way of loving and moving through the world is valid and real.

And yes, part of her joy came from a random TikTok scroll late one evening. But that's how queer magic works sometimes. Each time someone finds the right words, each time they speak their truth into the world, they take one step closer to wholeness. And in that wholeness, queer joy blooms.

Mandy's story is a beautiful example of what happens when a queer person accepts themselves for who they are and when the people around them celebrate their identity.

But what happens when coming out isn't so easy?

Mason's Story

Coming Out to Yourself

Mason grew up in a world where every step of his future was already mapped out. Raised in a conservative Christian home, his life was supposed to follow a straight and narrow path: Christian school,

Christian college, a future in ministry, marriage to a nice Christian girl, and raising a godly family. From the outside, it looked like he was on track. But inside, he was struggling.

In high school, Mason began to realize he was attracted to other boys. He was terrified. This wasn't part of the plan. Night after night, he prayed for the feelings to disappear, believing they were sinful, a test, or a temptation. He threw himself into schoolwork, rising to the top of his class. In college, he stayed just as focused. He distracted himself with Bible studies, student government, and packed schedules... anything to avoid answering questions about why he wasn't dating.

But Mason was lonely. He had no one he trusted enough to confide in, no one who knew what was truly going on inside him. He feared that even whispering his truth aloud might destroy the life he had built.

Then, one day, a busload of queer Christian activists arrived on campus. They were part of the Equality Ride, a group advocating for LGBTQ+ students at Christian colleges. At first, Mason was skeptical. But curiosity overpowered fear, and he started asking questions. What he heard changed everything. These people were also Christians, and they believed that being queer wasn't a curse or a sin. It was a gift.

That encounter sparked something in him. He began reading about theology, sexuality, and the Bible's deeper messages of love and liberation. He found a secular therapist who helped him navigate the shame he had internalized. Slowly, Mason began to believe he could be both gay and beloved by God. By graduation, he wasn't just surviving anymore, he was ready to start coming out.

Coming Out to Others

Mason knew the road ahead wouldn't be easy. He began by telling two childhood friends. Their reaction was cautious, confused. "Have you tried praying it away?" they asked.

"I've prayed," he told them. "I've prayed harder than you can imagine. And after years of prayer, study, and therapy, I've finally found peace."

They tried to understand, but over time, their friendship faded.

Coming out to his family was even more difficult. He rehearsed the conversation in his head for weeks, agonizing over what to say, when to say it, and whether they'd still love him afterward. Eventually, he decided to say it all at once. At a family dinner, with his parents and siblings gathered around, he stood up, tears in his eyes, and told them the truth.

The room went still. His parents were stunned. This wasn't who their "golden boy" was supposed to be.

"We'll always love you," they said carefully. "But we don't know if we can ever accept this."

It was an imperfect, painful beginning. But with time, the conversations continued. They wrestled with their faith, with scripture, and with what love truly meant.

Living Authentically as Your Full Self

Life after coming out was both freeing and lonely. Mason lost many of the relationships that had once defined him. However, he found new ones that nourished him more deeply than he ever thought possible. He discovered queer community. He found a church that not only accepted him, but celebrated him. His faith began to bloom again, this time rooted in grace, not fear.

Then came Jimmy.

They met through a dating app, and something just clicked. What started as casual messages turned into late-night phone calls, romantic dates, and soon they were moving in together. Mason's family watched as he fell in love. Slowly, they began to open their hearts and Jimmy became a regular presence at family dinners.

Years later, Mason's brothers stood beside him at the altar while his parents, tearful and proud, sat in the front row cheering him on. He had done the impossible: not just coming out, but building a life filled with love, joy, faith, and family on his own terms.

Final Thoughts on Coming Out

Mason's story has a happy ending, but not all coming out stories do. For many people, coming out can carry real risks. For those raised in deeply homophobic or abusive environments, there is the risk of being disowned or even facing violence. That's why coming out is a deeply personal choice. If you're not ready, or if it doesn't feel safe, that's okay. Your worth isn't dependent upon disclosure.

You can still embrace who you are wholeheartedly, whether you are out to your family or not. You don't need to be out to your friends, your workplace, or your spiritual community in order to love or accept yourself. In the next chapter, we will explore ways you can take ownership of your own emotional well-being, and how that leads to finding queer joy.

Self-Esteem, Self-Compassion, and Self-Acceptance

Many people think that joy is something that comes *after*. *After* we've come out. *After* we've been accepted. *After* we've found a community, begun dating, or transitioned. But queer joy doesn't have to wait for the perfect moment… it's always within us.

Before I came out, I found queer joy in seeing my best friend fall in love with his first boyfriend. I felt it when I watched Willow and Tara's blossoming relationship on *Buffy the Vampire Slayer* and when Megan realized she was "a homo" in *But I'm a Cheerleader*. Queer joy was in the rush I felt as I wrote in my school journal about a book I had just read. I revealed how it resonated with me because the main character was bisexual and I thought that I might be too. It multiplied when I read the kind, affirming message my 11th-grade English teacher had written in the margins after she saw my journal entry. Queer joy isn't just about being seen by others. It's about seeing yourself, and choosing to love yourself for who you are. Jeffrey Borenstein, President of the Brain & Behavior Research Foundation, wrote:

> Self-love is a state of appreciation for oneself that grows from actions that support our physical, psychological and spiritual growth. Self-love means having a high regard for your own

well-being and happiness. Self-love means taking care of your own needs and not sacrificing your well-being to please others.[1]

While researching self-love, I've found it compared with self-esteem, self-compassion, and self-acceptance.

- **Self-esteem** is about how you value yourself. It's believing that you're worthy of kindness, of love, of respect. When you believe you're worthy, you allow yourself to feel joy without having to earn it first. In fact, "a voluminous body of research has shown that high self-esteem helps individuals adapt to and succeed in a variety of life domains, including having more satisfying relationships, performing better at school and work, enjoying improved mental and physical health, and refraining from antisocial behavior.[2]"
- **Self-compassion** is about accepting yourself even when things are hard. It's being gentle with yourself when you make mistakes and loving yourself through the pain. When you are hurting, self-compassion creates space to believe that you deserve healing, love, and joy. "In general, self-compassion entails displaying a positive and healthy attitude to the self, which enables the individual to deal effectively with the usual setbacks in human existence.[3]"
- **Self-acceptance** is the way that you feel when you recognize and embrace who you are. It's the feeling you get when you see yourself as a whole person, flaws and all, and you make peace with your authentic self. When you can find that acceptance, it creates space for you to believe you are worthy of experiencing joy!

---

1. Borenstein, J. "Self-Love and What It Means." *Brain & Behavior Research Foundation*, February 12, 2020. https://bbrfoundation.org/blog/self-love-and-what-it-means.
2. Orth, Ulrich, and Richard W. Robins. "Is High Self-Esteem Beneficial? Revisiting a Classic Question." *American Psychologist* 77, no. 1 (January 2022): 5–17. https://doi.org/10.1037/amp0000922.
3. Muris, Paul, and Henk Otgaar. "Self-Esteem and Self-Compassion: A Narrative Review and Meta-Analysis on Their Links to Psychological Problems and Well-Being." *Psychology Research and Behavior Management* 16 (August 3, 2023): 2961–2975. https://doi.org/10.2147/PRBM.S402357.

Believing in your worth, treating yourself with care, and embracing who you are are qualities that you control. They don't require you to be out of the closet or living up to anyone else's standards.

In the next three sections, we'll explore practices to help you cultivate self-love, resilience, and queer joy!

Mosaic Tile One
Red—Life / Self-Love

In the traditional Pride flag, the color red represents Life. Celebrating our joy is an essential part of being alive. For this mosaic tile, you are invited to reflect on the following questions, and then create a tile that represents the color red and the joy of living.

Prompt:

- Where can I find queer joy in the depth of my being?
- What makes me feel most *alive*?
- What part of my identity have I learned to love after once hiding it?

Creative Exercise:

Create an image or symbol to represent your life force. Maybe it's a heartbeat, a flame, or a spiral. Use red to reflect boldness, courage, and authenticity. This tile represents your breath, your pulse, and your very existence as a sacred being.

Example:

In this tile I chose to draw a red rose as the symbol of my life force. It mirrors my own queer journey from a bud that was rooted in tenderness and shaped by resilience into a blossom standing strong in bold defiance of what tried to keep me from growing.

How to Love Yourself

Over the years, I have worked with many queer people who have struggled with loving themselves. This is frequently caused by negative messages from society, family, friends, and faith communities. For example, someone might hear their coworker say that they don't care if they're gay, but they wish gay people wouldn't "shove it in their face all the time." This can lead them to start worrying that they might be talking about their life too often, being too honest, or being too gay.

Each of us carries internalized beliefs that we have inherited from others. For example, maybe someone told you that you were too much, or, on the contrary, that you'd never be enough. Maybe the people who were supposed to love you demonstrated that their love was conditional. Maybe your faith community said you had to choose between loving God and living authentically as your whole self. Maybe you have been conditioned to believe that you aren't good enough, aren't normal enough, and aren't lovable *as you are*.

We can begin to find self-love when we ask ourselves questions about these internalized beliefs. These questions might look like:

- Who told me this?
- What did they gain by influencing my beliefs? What has maintaining these beliefs cost me?
- Do I still want to carry this with me?

If the answer to that last question is no, then it's time to work on letting go of that negative belief.

One of the most powerful ways to change the way you think is to change the way you speak to yourself. When you internalize negative beliefs about who you are, those negative beliefs become an inner voice that is constantly critiquing you. RuPaul calls this voice his "Inner Saboteur[1]" and Brené Brown calls it her "Inner Gremlin[2]." I call mine the "Joy Thief," because my inner critic is constantly trying to steal my joy.

Sometimes, my Joy Thief can be a real jerk. She tells me that I am too queer and that people simply "tolerate" my existence. She tells me that I shouldn't be a parent and that my son is going to suffer from growing up with two moms. She tells me that I am not a good enough writer and that no one will want to read my book. She tells me that I am a failure for leaving my work as a minister, and that I am going to keep failing at everything I do.

At first, I believed all of the terrible things that my Joy Thief was telling me. It's a lot easier to accept those negative thoughts than it is to fight them. In my years doing pastoral care and coaching, I have listened to numerous people describe why they struggle with self-love. This has made me realize that we all have our own version of that inner critic. It is up to us to do the work to quiet our Joy Thief so we can finally live our best lives.

After realizing this, I decided to try a little experiment. For a full week, anytime I heard my Joy Thief criticizing something about me, I wrote it down on a piece of paper. Every night, I read those criticisms and would cross them out and replace them with something positive instead. I started calling this part of myself my "Joy Keeper" because it was the aspect that I needed to help me stand up against the Joy Thief.

Now, years later, when I hear that voice telling me I'm not enough, that I'm too queer, that I'm not worthy of love, I know my Joy Thief is back… and I know that I can ask my Joy Keeper for help.

You can do this too.

If a week feels like too much time, start by doing it for a day. Write

---

1. RuPaul. *The Gospel According to RuPaul: How to Be Universal*. New York: Gallery Books, 2019,
2. Brown, Brené. *The Gifts of Imperfection*. Center City, MN: Hazelden, 2010,

down each time you feel something negative toward yourself, and then reframe it into a positive.

Example: "My haircut is too butch."
Reframe: "My haircut is an authentic expression of who I am."

It's that simple. When we remove the things that are blocking us from loving ourselves, we make space for our authentic selves to show up. When we are no longer afraid to be our true selves, the door opens to experiencing joy.

If you are looking for ways to bring more self-love into your life, here are some options to consider:

- **Starting therapy**—A good therapist will help you explore the areas where you could use some extra help and then come up with a treatment plan to address those areas. If you are struggling with anxiety, depression, or trauma, therapy is a great place to feel supported as you work on healing.
- **Creating a Self-Care Routine**—Self-care encompasses more than taking bubble baths (though baths are actually a great way to relax and focus on your own needs). Self-care is anything that helps you feel happier and healthier– mentally, physically, emotionally, and spiritually. Eating healthy foods that nourish your body, getting enough sleep, exercising (as you are able), spending time in nature, listening to music, and meditating are all ways that you can add more self-care into your life.
- **Setting Boundaries**—Loving yourself also means prioritizing your needs. If there are people in your life who make hurtful comments or are harmful to your mental and emotional well-being, it is okay to set boundaries with them in order to protect yourself from harm.
- **Embracing Your Personal Expression**—What clothes feel good on your body? What haircut feels most affirming for you? What are the things that you wear that make you feel the most **you?** When we style ourselves in ways that make us feel like our authentic selves, it can spark our joy. Leaning in and accepting who you are helps your self-love grow.

- **Creating a Self-Love Journal**—Write down all the things that you love about yourself and keep them as a reminder that you can read when you are having a hard day.
- **Celebrating Queer Culture**—There is a rich diversity of books, movies, TV shows, musicians, artists, drag queens, poets, and other performers that lift up and celebrate our community. Intentionally seeking out queer media can help you discover what you love about being queer.
- **Working with a Coach or Spiritual Director**—If you need a little extra help empowering your Joy Keeper, disempowering your Joy Thief, or finding your joy, working with someone who is empathetic and has the tools to support you as you heal might be a great option for you.

Working with the right coach offers you a safe space to get to know who you truly are and to love yourself in the process. In my coaching work, I walk alongside folks who are learning to trust themselves, love themselves, and find their joy. I offer a calming presence, compassionate listening, and tools for reflection and self-growth. In the past, I have worked with people like:

- Emily, who was sick and tired of hiding who they were as a non-binary person and needed help finding the courage to be themself.
- Robert, who wanted to experience queer joy without shame, but didn't know where to start.
- Josie, who was raised in a religious home and needed support coming out and reconciling her faith with her identity.

Together, we shared experiences like:

- Naming inherited negative beliefs and internalized homophobia/transphobia and exploring how to rewrite them.
- Recognizing when the Joy Thief was at work and welcoming the Joy Keeper instead.
- Cultivating space for joy to be something felt, not earned.

- Using creative tools to foster self-love, self-esteem, and self-acceptance.
- Exploring spiritual healing through meditation, Tarot, and Reiki.

Whether you're ready to work with a coach or just starting to ask questions, I want you to know this: *Queer joy is not something you have to earn, it is always within you. Sometimes, you just need a little help finding it… and that's okay.*

The Self-Love Toolkit

Through my work as an Interfaith Minister of Queer Joy & Creative Liberation, I have spent years working with queer people who are on a journey towards self-love and healing. I offer one-on-one coaching, workshops, self-led retreats, and group retreats that help queer people find what they love about being queer, and then celebrating it.

A few years ago, I was contacted by Amy, a queer writer who was struggling with a major depressive episode after the publication of one of her books. I began doing Tarot readings for her twice a year, working with her on strategies to help her foster more self-love and self-compassion. Amy did a lot of important work based on our sessions together, and her mental health improved greatly.

After working together for a couple of years, Amy decided to get a bonus reading before a major book tour. Her book was focused on difficult topics such as homophobia and sexism, which she would be discussing at each event. She was worried that the stress of the book tour and the emotional cost of her events might result in her depression returning.

It was a valid concern, and I wanted to make sure that I did what I could to help. After a couple of Tarot spreads to help us with direction, we worked together to create a beautiful self-care ritual that she could do after each event. This ritual allowed her to honor the experience of each stop on her tour and then release it, rather than internalizing the heavy emotions that came up during the events. Thanks to this ritual, she completed the tour invigorated, empowered, and inspired. When she finished, she shared that this book tour was full of queer joy because she was able to truly celebrate the experience.

Small rituals can hold tremendous power. Over the years, I have developed or adopted several tools which can help people to find self-love and self-affirmation. These are not intended to be a replacement for traditional therapy, but they are helpful ways to explore, play, and invoke queer joy.

Want to find your joy? Here are a few tools that you can try on your own:

TOOL ONE: The Self-Love Altar

- **Purpose:** To create a sacred space of self-affirmation.
- **Suggested Supplies:** Candle, Photos (a childhood photo or photo of you at a Pride event would be great options), rose quartz, flowers, incense, written affirmations, a love letter to yourself, or any items of significance.
- **How-To:** I recommend finding a small, flat surface to create your altar on. Place photos, objects, affirmations, and candles on the altar. You can do this simply with just one or two small items, or you can make an ornate altar with many different reminders of self-love and pride. Visit it daily to meditate, say a short affirmation, or even pray. Use it in the way that feels most healing and life-giving for you.

TOOL TWO: Gratitude Lists

When researcher Brené Brown was studying the topic of joy, she discovered that the best way to find joy is to focus on gratitude. In an interview with Marie Kondo, Brown explained,

"In the research, we learned that the most effective way to cultivate joy in our lives is to practice gratitude. The key word here is practice. It's not just about *feeling* grateful, it's about developing an observable practice. So often we think that joy makes us grateful, when in reality it's gratitude that brings joy."[1]

- **Purpose:** To orient your day toward joy and presence.
- **How-To:** Each morning or evening, write down three things you're grateful for. These can be big or small. Include queer-specific gratitude whenever you can. Example: *chosen family, gender euphoria, a good pronoun day.* I recommend keeping this as a running list on your phone, or in a little note-pad somewhere special in your home, so you can look back on it whenever you need a little extra joy.

TOOL THREE: Mirror Work

Mirror work can be a powerful tool to boost your self-love and self-esteem. It may feel awkward at first, but if you can keep going it might just be what you need.

- **Purpose:** To practice self-recognition and appreciation.
- **How-To:** Look into your own eyes in the mirror and say something kind. Start with: "I am worthy," or "I'm proud of how far I've come." You can even write on the mirror with a dry erase marker or on post-it notes to remind yourself of these affirming words. Repeat as often as you need.

TOOL FOUR: Love Letter to Self

- **Purpose:** To name your worth and offer it back to yourself.
- **How-To:** Write a letter to yourself that begins with: "Dear [Chosen Name], I love you because…" Be as tender and bold as you can. Include what loving yourself looks and feels like.
- **Optional:** You can seal it in an envelope and keep it on hand to read when you need a pick-me-up.

---

1. Brené Brown. "Brené Brown Interview." *KonMari* (blog), [n.d.], https://konmari.com/brene-brown-interview/?srsltid=AfmBOorbk7MNMgzYiMjUdUqMGiclcLBt8y_M6tuUXXsapDfqRM7J0d_W (accessed June, 15th, 2025).

TOOL FIVE: Queer Affirmations

- **Purpose:** To internalize joyful identity.
- **How-To:** Speak or write affirmations daily. Try:
  - "I am proud to be pansexual and I am worthy of joy."
  - "My transness is sacred."
  - "I do not need to shrink to be lovable."

This toolkit isn't complete without *your* voice. What self-love practice brings *you* queer joy?

TOOL NAME: _____

Purpose: _____

How-To: _____

Conclusion

In this chapter, we've explored some of the internal factors that influence how and when we feel queer joy. Loving ourselves is revolutionary. So much of our society tries to hide us or make us feel ashamed of who we are. Self-love gives us the power to keep going, to keep growing, and to find our joy.

Throughout this section, I have given you several tools for finding and nurturing your self-love. This is an invitation: choose one of these tools today and commit to it. Whether it is fighting back against your joy thief, building a self-love altar, or writing yourself a love letter, each choice you make is a positive move forward.

The road to queer joy is built one bold, loving step at a time. Take yours.

Questions for Reflection:

- What small moments of joy do I notice in my daily life?
- What affirmations or self-reminders help me combat negativity and reclaim joy?
- What self-care practices make me feel the most affirmed in my identity?
- How do I use personal expression (fashion, music, art, etc.) to celebrate my identity?
- What is one way I can incorporate more joy into my self-care routine this week?

Mosaic Tile Two
Orange—Healing

In the traditional Pride flag, the color orange represents Healing. Healing is an essential part of finding our queer joy. For this mosaic tile, you are invited to reflect on the following questions and then create a tile that represents the color orange and finding joy in your healing journey.

Prompt:

- What have I healed from, or am still healing from?
- Who or what has helped me feel whole again?
- What would I say if I could write a note of compassion to my past self?

Creative Exercise:

Use orange to depict warmth and resilience. Maybe it's a cracked vessel mended with gold, a sunset, or your own hand reaching back in time. Let this tile honor your healing journey and how it has shaped your joy.

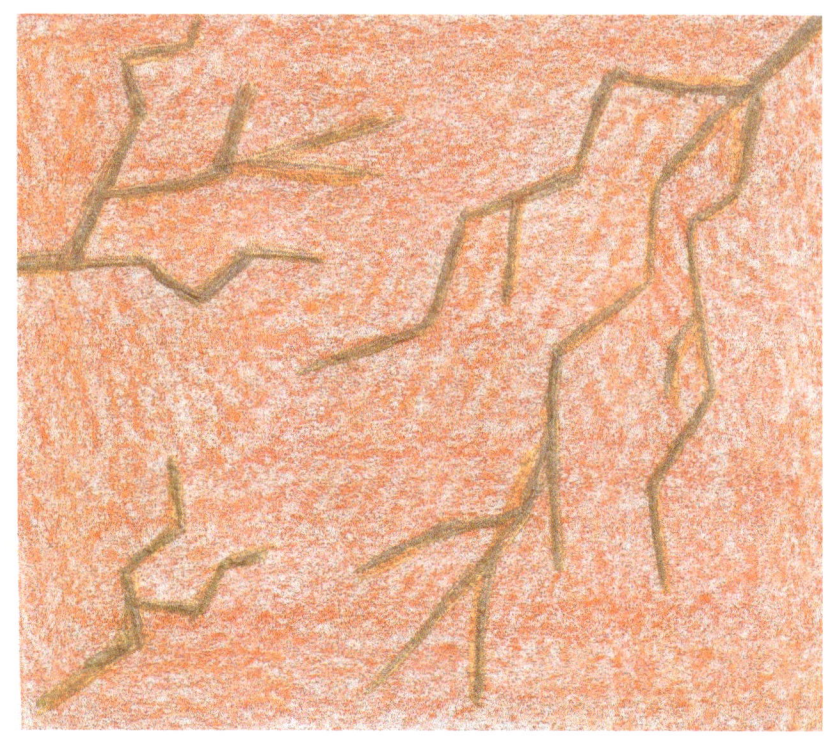

Example:

In this tile, I created an orange background that was intentionally marked with visible cracks. The orange holds the warmth of life, creativity, and endurance, while the cracks tell the truth of what has been broken along the way. I filled those fractures with golden threads as an homage to the kintsugi tradition of honoring not just repair, but the sacred beauty of healing itself.

Section 3

Finding Community

"What is family? Most would say family means a group of people closely related by blood or marriage as parents, children, uncles, aunts, and cousins. This is family of the biological kind. By the same token I've learned in my life experience that family can also be of the chosen kind. As queer people we very often find that our chosen families are the ones who love us unconditionally and pick up the slack in support of our personal truths and humanity when our biological family members don't have the tools."

— Billy Porter, Unprotected: A Memoir

"Bethany is one of my closest friends, and my entire family considers her to be part of our family. We went to high school and college together, and she even lived with my husband, Jason, and me for several years. She has been there for graduations, funerals, and family vacations. Bethany is like my sister, even though we aren't related by blood."

Matt's voice cracked as he raised his beer and continued with his best man speech. I looked over at my wife sitting next to me at the bridal table, and she smiled and squeezed my hand gently. The lights hanging from the pavilion twinkled overhead. A cool autumn breeze swept through, rustling the artificial flowers and loosening strands of the mermaid-colored hair that had escaped from my up-do.

It hadn't been long since the pavilion was full of the hustle and bustle of our family moving furniture, putting up pictures, and laying out decorations. We were in the midst of a worldwide pandemic, so we had been forced to make some difficult changes to our original wedding plan. The date changed from October 2020 to the following year. The guest list had been cut in half, with many of our friends and family watching the ceremony on Zoom instead of attending in person. There was no wedding planner, no formal seating chart, no rigorous schedule to maintain. It was just us and the people who love us.

Our wedding guests were a patchwork quilt of the people who meant the most to us, stitched together across time zones and decades. Our out-of-state family traveled from all over the country to be there, crossing state lines and navigating pandemic concerns to witness our special day. Our local family showed up hours early to turn a simple park pavilion into a space for celebration. We are blessed to have biological families who love and support both of us.

We are also blessed to have an incredible amount of chosen family.

My best friends from Michigan made up my wedding party. I've known them since I was a twelve-year-old theatre kid who was just starting to find my voice. Among them were Matt and Jason. They were my very first roommates, and they've been with me through every formative moment of my life. They've seen every single part of me and loved me anyway.

Katie, another one of my dearest friends from Michigan, flew in too. Katie's the kind of friend who shows up for the people she loves.

From attending my dad's funeral to dancing down the aisle as our flower girl, I always know I can count on her.

My seminary cohort, affectionately known as "The Avengers," arrived in full force. "Iron Man" even officiated our ceremony, grounding it in the kind of fierce, funny, sacred energy that only a group of slightly irreverent ministers could muster.

Our Kansas friends made sure everything ran smoothly. Chad ran the Zoom so our loved ones could attend virtually. Geneva, Kelsee's maid of honor, brought creativity and passion to every detail. Naphtali showed up in a dinosaur costume just as we started taking pictures, bringing the levity and laughter that made our day so special.

It was our wedding day, but it was also much more than that. We were witnessed. Held. Celebrated by the ones who love us the most. We stood in the center of a circle of people who had seen us through heartbreaks and comings-outs, through cross-country moves and late-night breakdowns. People who had been there for us throughout our lives, and who, even in the midst of a pandemic, still showed up for us. They showed up with masks, and pies, dance moves… and radiant, immeasurable joy!

Finding Support

Maya Angelou once wrote, "We need joy as we need air. We need love as we need water. We need each other as we need the earth we share.[1]"

In the previous section, we discussed the ways queer people find joy through internal work. When we focus on healing ourselves, we allow our joy to fill the places that once were full of self-doubt, insecurity, and internalized queerphobia. Our journey toward joy starts internally, but it continues as we connect with the people around us. We are not meant to live this life alone. Queer joy flourishes in connection with people who understand us, affirm us, and walk beside us through the highs and lows.

When the world feels isolating or hostile, finding and building supportive networks is an essential part of our survival. Whether it's a friend who sees your whole self, a faith community that affirms your dignity, or an ally who speaks up when it matters, these relationships remind us that we belong. They remind us that we matter. They remind us that we are not alone.

Even if you do not have supportive family or queer friends in your local area, there is power in connecting with others through social media and other online resources. In this section, we will be exploring

---

1. Maya Angelou, *Phenomenal Woman: Four Poems Celebrating Women* (New York: Random House, 1995),

the many different ways that queer people can find joy by connecting with their community.

Family of Origin

When my colleague Robin's eight-year-old daughter came out as transgender, it happened on an ordinary Sunday afternoon. Robin was playing with her kiddos outside when Hayden ran up to her and said, "Mommy, I'm a girl."

It was as simple as that.

Robin was not surprised by this revelation, but she was surprised by the confidence that coming out gave Hayden. Before, Hayden was timid in new spaces, worried about what other people would think of her. Now, she greeted the people around her with excitement. She was still the same funny, creative, curious kid, but now she seemed more comfortable in her own skin.

Just as the family was settling into their new normal, they discovered that they were no longer safe in their own home. Their state's legislature had been working relentlessly to pass anti-trans laws, including bans on gender-affirming care for minors and prohibiting trans girls from playing sports. The message was clear: the state was targeting her child simply for existing. The family made a heartbreaking choice: they left their home and community and moved to a state that had legal protections for their daughter.

In the midst of all this, Robin and her spouse encouraged their kids to find joy in the simple moments. They went blueberry picking, marched in parades, and played silly games at home. She told me,

"The times that we can celebrate joy and the gift of transness are all the more important and meaningful to us as a family."

For Robin, the "gift of transness" is seeing her daughter refuse to accept stereotypes or limitations on her gender. It is the courage that her daughter shows in her daily life, and the freedom with which she has become her true self.

Robin also became an advocate for other families like hers. When parents ask what to do if their child comes out as trans, Robin answers: take a deep breath. Find community. Learn the language you need. Get your own support so your child doesn't carry the weight of your processing.

Robin's hope for the future is simple and profound: a world where queer and trans kids are treated like any other child. Until then, their family will raise their daughters with love, delight, and fierce protection, knowing that joy is not only a gift but an act of resistance.

Family is (in most cases) our first example of love and connection with other people. They are the people who bring us into this world, who nurture us as we grow, and who help shape us into the people we will become. Under the right conditions, family can be our strongest allies and advocates. However, family can also be complicated and messy. After all, you don't get to choose who your relatives are.

When queer people come out, the reactions from our family of origin can range from exuberant affirmation to abusive and traumatic rejection. These reactions, and the subsequent behaviors of family members toward their queer relatives, can have a profound impact on our lives.

The Family Acceptance Project based out of San Francisco State University has been studying queer families for over 20 years. In their research, they found that teenagers and young adults who were supported when they came out as queer or trans were healthier than those who were not supported. They had stronger mental health, higher self-esteem, and were less likely to use drugs. They also found:

> ...when gay and transgender youth were accepted by their families, they were much more likely to believe they would

have a good life and would be a happy, productive adult. In families that were not at all accepting of their adolescent's gay or transgender identity, only about 1 in 3 young people thought they would have a good life as a gay adult. But in families that were extremely accepting, almost all LGBT young people thought they would have a good life.[1]

When our families accept, affirm, and celebrate us, we benefit. For the most part, I am blessed to have a loving, close family who fully accept my identity as a queer person and my marriage to my wife. My Mom was one of the first people I came out to when I was 16 years old, and from that moment she has been one of my fiercest allies. My step-dad, siblings, and the majority of my extended family have also been wonderfully accepting toward me and our other queer relatives. My in-laws welcomed me into their family with open arms and have been very supportive of my relationship with my wife.

The family members I am closest with have all had a positive influence on my journey. Through these relationships, I have learned that having a family that supports you as an LGBTQ+ person can help you feel safe, secure, and loved. Affirming families provide a space where you can be your authentic self without fear of rejection. This can significantly reduce minority stress, anxiety, and the mental health challenges that are so often linked to discrimination. It can help foster greater self-love, self-esteem, and self-acceptance. It can also reinforce the truth that your identity is valid and worth celebrating. Affirmation and validation from our biological families are a powerful source of queer joy!

On the other hand, the Family Acceptance Project learned that gay and trans teenagers and young adults who were not accepted by their families had lower self-esteem and were more isolated from their community. They also found that:

> Gay and transgender teens who were highly rejected by their parents and caregivers were at very high risk for health and

---

1. Family Acceptance Project. *Supportive Families, Healthy Children.* Accessed [insert date]. https://familyproject.sfsu.edu/sites/default/files/documents/FAP_English%20Booklet_pst.pdf.

mental health problems when they become young adults (ages 21-25). Highly rejected young people were:

- More than 8 times as likely to have attempted suicide
- Nearly 6 times as likely to report high levels of depression
- More than 3 times as likely to use illegal drugs, and
- More than 3 times as likely to be at high risk for HIV and sexually transmitted diseases[2]

When family does not support you as an LGBTQ+ person, the impact can be deeply harmful. When our loved ones tell us that they do not accept and affirm our identities, their voices can become the internalized message that tells us that we are wrong, that we are bad, that we should be ashamed of who we are.

I know this from personal experience. While the majority of my family is supportive, I also have relatives who have not supported my queer identity or my relationship. The last time I saw my grandpa he told me that he hated all gay people and if I was gay, that included me. I am grateful we reconciled over the phone when he was on his deathbed, but even a decade later that statement still hurts.

For much of my dad's life, he was an anti-gay activist. He believed that being gay was a sin, and he was very loud about this belief. While I was in the process of coming out, I assumed that when my dad found out I was queer we would no longer have a relationship. While I was out to almost everyone else in my life, I went back into the closet every time I visited my dad's house. This continued for seven years, until I finally decided that I was tired of hiding. I told my dad that I was gay, and he replied that he would always love me even if he didn't "agree with my lifestyle."

Rejection from loved ones often leads to feelings of isolation, shame, and self-doubt, making it harder to feel safe in your own identity. When I was visiting my dad, I was never fully comfortable. While I was a minor, I was concerned that he would find out I was gay and try to send me to conversion therapy. Even as an adult I would watch my language, my mannerisms, and the stories I would tell him about my life, all in an effort to appear "less gay."

---

2. Family Acceptance Project, *Supportive Families*.

My relationship with my dad shifted and grew in the years after I came out to him. He passed away in 2018, but in the years leading up to his death he was becoming more and more accepting... he even began to ask me about how my girlfriend was doing when I would talk to him on the phone. I watched him soften and become more accepting over time. To this day, I mourn that my dad never had a chance to meet my wife or see me living as my full, authentic self.

When you have a family member that does not accept you for who you are, you are often forced to ask hard questions about what that means for your relationship. Some choose to keep their relationship the same and either stay in the closet or tiptoe around their identity to stay safe. Others may remove themselves completely from being in relationship with that person for the sake of their own mental health. For many, a third option is drawing clear boundaries that allow them to continue to be in one another's lives while also prioritizing their own mental and emotional health. All of these are valid choices, it is up to each individual to decide what makes the most sense for them.

My mom was married to my sister's father from the time I was a baby until I was in middle school. He is the man who raised me through my most formative years, and he still holds a place in my heart. However, he is a very conservative Christian and believes that being gay is a sin. Since I came out in high school, our relationship has been... complicated.

We have drawn boundaries, and with those boundaries we both feel safe enough to remain in each other's lives. We do not discuss politics and rarely discuss religion. While he refused to attend my wedding, he treats my wife with respect and loves his grandson. Our relationship is not always easy to maintain, it takes work. Sometimes it is painful, sometimes it is frustrating, and sometimes I want to give up on it altogether. However, I have found that when we are both able to stick to our boundaries, we find a middle ground where we can laugh over a shared meal, play with my son, and enjoy each other's company.

Remember, **you** control your relationships. You can choose what treatment you will accept from others and what behaviors you will not accept in your life. If you find that the people around you are stealing your joy, you have the power to draw clearer boundaries or remove yourself from the situation altogether.

When your biological family cannot be your main source of support, it is important to remember that you have other people in your life who can be that support. In the next few chapters, we will explore more ways to find joy in the people and groups around us.

Chosen Family

My tarot client Michael grew up in a small, conservative town as a Mexican immigrant. Queerness wasn't discussed in his home or community. If queer people were present, they were quietly ignored or gossiped about in private. Without a supportive family and no one "like him" in his life, Michael often felt alienated and alone while he was growing up.

As an adult, through therapy, self-discovery, and coming out, Michael began to find himself. He began to intentionally surround himself with people who celebrated their queerness. He befriended folks who were unapologetically queer and trans. He also became selective about the spaces he entered, curating an inner circle that not only accepted but also affirmed him.

While he is no longer in a relationship with his family of origin, Michael has found a chosen family that he cares deeply for and who cares deeply for him. It is his chosen family who show up for the important milestones in his life. They celebrate holidays and birthdays together. They attended his graduation from college and his engagement party with his fiancée. And when he was in the hospital for a burst appendix, it was his chosen family who arrived with flowers and balloons and kept him company.

When he was growing up, Michael did not have access to any spaces that celebrated his queerness or opportunities to be with others like him. Today, he never misses a chance to attend Pride. He loves to see queer people travel from all over the state to access resources, spend time with their community, attend drag shows, listen to queer music, and dance. He didn't have that as a kid, but now that he does, he wants to help fill the world with more queer celebration and excellence!

He now describes his life as filled with individuals who "see joy in their queerness" and who reflect the same radical celebration he offers them. These relationships sustain him, providing the support that his early environment could not. He has a family now, one that loves and affirms him just as he is.

One of the gifts of being queer is participating in the rich tradition of creating a chosen family. While you cannot choose the family that you are born into, you do have the power to choose who you surround yourself with. Dan Gemeinhart put it this way, "A found family is every bit as beautiful as a born family. Even more so, perhaps. Stories are about choices, after all, and to choose to be family is as wonderful a story as can be told.[1]"

These relationships can become some of the most important ones in your life. For those who have been rejected by biological relatives or simply need different kinds of connection, chosen family can be a strong system of support. These are the people who show up for us no matter what. They bring soup when we are sick. They cheer for us at drag shows and sit with us while we wait for doctor's appointments. They remind us that we are not alone. Kath Weston, an anthropologist and author of the book *Families We Choose*, "… described chosen family as deliberately chosen networks of support in LGBT communities, consisting of friends, partners and ex-partners, biological and nonbiological children, and others who provide kinship support.[2]"

The concept of chosen family may not seem unique to the queer community. Many people have close friendships that are so strong they

---

1. Dan Gemeinhart, *The Midnight Children* (New York: Scholastic Press, 2020)
2. Gates, T. "Chosen Families." In *The SAGE Encyclopedia of Marriage, Family, and Couples Counseling*, vol. 4, 240–242. SAGE Publications, 2017. https://doi.org/10.4135/9781483369532.n74.

feel like family. We often see this represented in popular tv shows like *Friends* and *How I Met Your Mother*. In these shows, we see important, meaningful friendships. They support each other through the good times and the bad, attend weddings and funerals, share holidays and celebrations, visit each other in the hospital, care for each other's children, and often show up when biological families cannot.

However, when it comes to the queer experience of having a chosen family, it's important to note that there are some key differences from the intimate friend groups we see on mainstream television. The friendships in shows like *Friends* are about companionship, not survival. Their relationships are strong and powerful, but they are not the same as the relationships found in a chosen family.

Chosen families often form out of necessity. They come together when biological families have rejected us or when we need understanding from people who have lived through similar experiences. In shows like *Pose, The L Word,* or *Rent*, the bonds are not just about who you want to grab a drink with after work. They are about who will show up for you when you're sick, who will affirm your identity when no one else will, and who will make sure you have a bed to sleep in. The stakes are higher, the care runs deeper, and the joy is more radical.

Queer chosen families are less about who we choose to spend time with and more about who helps us survive and live happier, healthier lives. For those of us on the margins, having close relationships with people who understand us is a powerful thing. One of my favorite examples of a queer chosen family is the community found in the X-Men comics and movies.

In the X-Men universe, mutants are misunderstood, discriminated against, and marginalized in their own communities. Through the invitation of Charles Xavier, these mutants find a home where they truly belong. Once they join the X-Men they can let go of the constant worry that the humans in their neighborhoods and workplaces will discover their identities. They have found somewhere that is safe with people who they can relate to. They don't have to hide who they are or try to prove that they are "one of the good mutants." They can simply be themselves.

For queer people, our families of choice give us this same freedom. With family or friends who are cisgender and heterosexual, we often have to navigate microaggressions or explain the importance of things like pronouns. Even when our straight and cisgender allies are doing their very best, feeling like we must constantly explain ourselves or answer questions can be exhausting. It is a beautiful thing when we can be around other people who share our experiences. When we are around our chosen family, we can be together without worrying about whether we are understood or accepted.

For many queer people, romantic relationships are a foundational part of our chosen families. When I met Kelsee, I knew that I had found the person who I was going to spend the rest of my life with. We laugh together, cry together, and dream together in beautiful ways. She is the person I want to wake up next to and the person I want to go to sleep with for the rest of my life—even when we have a screaming baby in the crib next to us. She is my person, the biggest source of my joy and my peace.

Loving, romantic partnerships can offer stability, companionship, and the possibility of a shared future. In a 2024 study of 484 long-term, married queer couples, the Williams Institute at UCLA School of Law found that:

> ...marriage improved their sense of safety and security (83%), life satisfaction (75%), and relationship stability (67%). In addition, marriage has influenced how same-sex couples support and depend on each other. Approximately one in five couples have contributed to each other's education costs, provided caregiving for health issues, disabilities, or aging, or relocated when their spouse got a new job.[3]

Feeling queer love openly and without shame is powerful and joyful. It affirms that our desire for companionship is a valid and beautiful part of the human experience. Experiencing joy and pleasure in queer intimacy can help us to heal from the wounds caused by societal stigma and to truly love ourselves.

Having chosen family is a beautiful part of the queer experience, but it is not the only way we can find queer joy in community. In the

---

3. Abbie E. Goldberg, *Perspectives on Marriage Equality in 2024* (Los Angeles: Williams Institute, UCLA School of Law, June 2024), https://williamsinstitute.law.ucla.edu/publications/marriage-equality-in-2024/.

next chapter, we will explore friendships, community relationships, and pride.

The Larger Queer Community

From large-scale Pride celebrations to local community gatherings, being with other LGBTQ+ people is an essential part of the queer experience. These events help foster a sense of belonging and give us greater visibility in a society that wants us to remain hidden. Connection with other queer people helps remind us that we are not alone, that we are part of a larger network of queer people all around the world.

In a 2024 academic study on the benefits of playing LGBTQ+ sports, the researchers found that "… people with more fully integrated LGBTQ identities, and greater club/team and LBGTQ+ community connectedness, reported better psychological health and well-being.[1]" They came to the conclusion that the benefits of being on a queer team were less about playing the sport itself, but rather about the kinship they found through playing it. They also concluded that Meyer's Minority Stress Theory was correct in asserting that "community support through the formation of social connections serves as a buffer against the negative effects of minority stress.[2]"

We have already explored the deep connections found in chosen

---

1. Anderson, Joel, Derrek J. Toussaint, and Adam Gerace. "An Exploration of the Psychological Benefits of Participation in LGBTQ Sport." *Aca J Spo Sci & Med* 2, no. 1 (2024). https://doi.org/10.33552/AJSSM.2024.02.000530.
2. Ibid.

family. This study shows that even everyday friendships and time spent with other queer people are vital sources of queer joy. Being with friends creates space for relationships, laughter, and peace. Even when connections within the queer community are casual, they hold a shared understanding of the queer experience. This sense of mutual recognition makes ordinary interactions feel easy and safe and decreases the negative effects of minority stress.

Queer joy flourishes in physical spaces that are intentionally designed to nurture it. LGBTQ+ friendly bookstores, coffee shops, community centers, and gay bars allow queer people to express themselves authentically without fear. They are places where people connect through shared art, conversation, or simply the comfort of being surrounded by affirming energy. They offer opportunities for us to celebrate our shared identities and to feel the collective experience of being with others like us. These spaces are places of safety where queerness is celebrated, not just tolerated.

For so many of us in the LGBTQ+ community, queer-affirming spaces have been our sanctuaries. A queer-owned café or a bookstore with a Pride flag in the window are places where we can safely relax with our community. As I have been writing this book, I have spent most of my time in a local, queer-forward coffee shop. They have rainbow flags on the walls, gender-neutral bathrooms, and flyers for queer events on the bulletin boards. When I am working on my laptop adorned with rainbow stickers, I feel like I fit right in!

A queer bar or nightclub can offer us a safe place to date, to dance, and to meet other queer people. My first queer nightclub experience was at Necto, in Ann Arbor, MI. In my late teens and early twenties, I spent many a Friday night with my friends dancing and singing and just letting loose on their dance floor. When it hasn't felt safe to show affection while on a date or with a significant other in public spaces, these places are a refuge from the outside world.

Pride Events

Every June, streets and parks around the world come alive with the colors and sounds of Pride. Pride began as a movement for liberation, and that energy still moves through every march, festival, and gathering. When we walk together, sing together, and celebrate together, we join a long line of people who have chosen authenticity over silence. Pride events ground us in the connection between the people who fought for queer rights in the past and the people who will continue that tradition into the future.

The first Pride marches in the 1970s commemorated the Stonewall Riots, a pivotal moment in LGBTQ+ history. Pride continues to remain a powerful demonstration of resilience, reminding the world that queer people refuse to be silenced or erased. It also serves as a space for collective joy, affirming queer identities through parades, festivals, and community engagement. Alongside the dancing, singing, and partying, there are also tables for advocacy, opportunities to register to vote, and resources for healthcare and mutual aid.

Research has shown that participating in Pride events has a positive impact on mental health and self-acceptance for LGBTQ+ individuals. A study by Riggle and Rostosky on mental health and the LGBTQ+ Community found that visibility at Pride leads to increased self-esteem and a stronger sense of belonging, particularly among those who may not have affirming communities elsewhere.[3]

As a queer activist, Pride celebrations have been central to my work. I have worked booths that advertised safe spaces for queer people in religious communities, collected signatures for fair housing in Kansas City, and advocated for reproductive justice in New Mexico. When I have attended Pride events, I have carried on Pride's political legacy by helping folks get registered to vote and connecting my family and clients with essential resources. Pride events are one of the best ways to learn about local non-profits and what they offer our community.

When I transitioned from working in churches to working for myself, my wife and I started taking our "Queer and Crafty" art business to Pride events. We found a tremendous amount of support for our work from queer people from all over New Mexico and Texas. In fact, art and creativity flow through Pride in the form of drag shows, performances, parade floats, and fashion. Queer-owned businesses and artists thrive at Pride markets, creating both community and economic empowerment.

---

3. Riggle, E. D. B., and S. S. Rostosky. "A Positive View of LGBTQ Identities: Implications for Mental Health and Well-Being." *Psychology & Sexuality*.

Large Pride parades and festivals are incredible sources of joy and celebration. When I first attended Pride in Chicago, I was surrounded by thousands of people waving Pride flags and dancing in the streets! I can still remember the feeling of freedom that I experienced as I was enveloped by the joyful energy of the queer and trans people all around me. In these moments, we know that we are not alone. We are surrounded by community, affirmed by non-profit organizations, and supported by allies who join us in solidarity.

Community Pride gatherings may be more intimate, but they are still very powerful. I have attended smaller Pride events in Michigan, Kansas, Missouri, New Mexico, and Texas and they each have something beautiful to offer the community. Most of these events are traditional festivals or Pride parades. In towns with fewer resources, Pride might also look like a picnic in the park, a poetry reading at the library, or a concert at the local UU church. The intimate nature of these events often creates space for deeper conversation and connection.

When people gather in smaller numbers with their local community, they often find new friendships and support networks that continue long after June. The simple act of being together, sharing food, and listening to one another creates a circle of belonging. Whether celebrated in a city street overflowing with people, or in a small-town park where a handful gather, Pride creates space for joy that heals and sustains us in more difficult times.

Mosaic Tile Three
Yellow—Sunlight

In the traditional Pride flag, the color yellow represents Sunlight. The people in our lives are often a source of light and joy in our lives. For this mosaic tile, you are invited to reflect upon the following questions and then create a tile that represents the color yellow and finding joy and light within your community.

Prompt:

- When have I felt truly seen and safe among other queer people?
- What spaces (physical or digital) have felt like sunlight to me?
- Who are my queer elders, chosen family, or companions?

Creative Exercise:

Let yellow radiate across this tile. Draw rays, circles, or overlapping silhouettes. You might collage photos, names, or phrases that remind you of people who light you up. This tile honors the warmth of your connection with others and the way our community can shine like sunlight on our paths.

Example:

In this tile, I chose to draw a yellow sun with rays radiating outward across the page. The bright, luminous colors represent the community that surrounds me with warmth and love and the people whose presence nourishes my spirit. The outward stretch of the rays mirror how care, joy, and belonging travel beyond a single source and ripple into everything they touch.

Virtual Events, Online Support, and Pop Culture

In-person events are great ways to connect with queer community, however, many people do not have access to in-person events. Folks who are still closeted, who live with disabilities, or who are located in small, rural areas may not be able to find or attend queer events. Thankfully, there are many ways to still connect with the queer community without leaving your house.

Queer Media and Pop Culture

One way to nurture queer joy from home is through queer media. Representation matters, and seeing ourselves reflected in art, music, film, and literature can be deeply affirming. Singers like Brandi Carlile, Chappell Roan, Janelle Monae, and Sam Smith reflect our lives and our experiences in their lyrics and melodies. Their work gives our community music that unites us at queer events, provides love songs for our engagement and wedding celebrations, and helps us feel less alone.

TV shows and movies with authentic queer characters help us see ourselves reflected on the screen. When I was growing up, couples like Willow and Tara, Graham and Megan, and Bette and Tina gave me examples of what queer love could look like. Today, TV shows and movies like *Heartstopper, RuPaul's Drag Race, Pose,* and *Love, Simon* show us as real people in all sorts of storylines and situations. Queer art, books, and podcasts lift up queer stories and content. All of this representation is essential because it shows us that our lives and our stories matter.

Virtual Community

One of the most beautiful things about modern technology is that we are now able to connect with other queer folks in ways we could not have imagined just 20 or 30 years ago! Today, queer community, support, and information are never more than a few clicks away. Virtual spaces give us 24/7 access to online forums, Discord servers, and group chats that are always open and available. Social media platforms like TikTok, Facebook, Instagram, and YouTube support queer creators who share their content with the broader community.

For many people, a virtual community is a safe place to explore. These online spaces provide a sense of anonymity and affirmation for folks who want to try out new names, pronouns, or identities before sharing them in everyday life. There's something powerful about typing out "my name is ___" or "my pronouns are ___" in a supportive online group and receiving immediate affirmation.

Virtual communities also give us the chance to build chosen family across the country or even throughout the world. For folks who do not have many offline queer friendships, relationships that are forged online can be just as meaningful. I have met people online who have become dear friends, and I have met people in real life whom I now only interact with virtually. These connections remind us that no matter how far apart we may be physically, we are never alone.

Beyond these more casual virtual communities, there are also structured online events that bring queer folks together. These range from workshops, classes, and retreats to virtual conferences that draw people from across the globe. You only need to do a quick Google search to be connected with queer book clubs, online support groups, and discussion circles. Some organizations even host online Pride celebrations. I have found great connection and support in several of these virtual spaces. When I have been unable to afford to travel for a conference, having a virtual option for attendance has helped me to participate in more accessible ways. I have participated in online workshops, retreats, classes, and book clubs. I have also found community in virtual queer writing and spirituality groups.

Perhaps most importantly, I have found support as a queer parent on social media. Hearing stories from other queer families on TikTok and Instagram helped my wife and I feel less alone as we began our journey towards parenthood. As our son's non-biological parent, I found encouragement from others who have lived through the same experience. I even found the lawyer who helped complete my second-parent adoption through a Facebook group! I was excited to share her information with other queer parents who also needed to adopt their child, and to support other new parents in the same ways I have been supported.

Being physically distant from an affirming queer community doesn't mean you have to be isolated. Your community is out there—it just might look different from what you expected. Whether through a Discord chat, a Zoom workshop, a TikTok feed, or a queer movie, there are countless ways to feel connected and affirmed.

The Relational Toolkit

Throughout this section, we have talked about many different ways to connect with affirming people around us. If you are struggling with how to start building authentic, supportive, joyful relationships, this section is for you!

In my work, I offer a variety of virtual ways to connect. I am the host of the *Joyfully Queer* podcast, which tells real stories of queer joy. I have led virtual gatherings, such as book clubs and crafting circles. I also offer workshops, retreats, and classes throughout the year that help queer folks and allies connect with their queer joy from the comfort of their own homes.

One way I am cultivating queer joy is through the Joyfully Queer Collective, a virtual gathering place designed for LGBTQ+ people who wish to root themselves in joy, connection, and creative expression. In this space, we connect through written posts, meditations, workshops, and community chats. Some weeks I might share a reflection or a guided meditation, while other weeks we gather for a live workshop on storytelling, spirituality, or creativity.

The rhythm of the Collective is intentionally gentle and sustainable, offering a balance of nourishment and connection. We celebrate one another's work, explore queer joy through art and story, and practice noticing joy in our daily lives. This is a place where group members are invited to be present, to contribute, and to remember that we are not alone. The Joyfully Queer Collective is a reminder that even in difficult times, we can choose to build spaces where joy is possible, and in doing so, we keep that joy alive for ourselves and each other.

Want to find joy in your community? Here are a few tools that you can try on your own:

TOOL: Mapping Your Joy Network

- **Purpose:** To discover who is in your supportive community.
- **How-To:** Grab a piece of paper or a journal. Draw a circle in the middle and write "My Queer Joy Network." Around it, write down names, groups, and places that currently bring you joy or where you'd like to build connections. Use different colors or symbols to mark family, chosen family, safe spaces, and community groups.

Reflection:
Where can I add new connections?
Which places or people might I reach out to this week?

TOOL: Queer Joy Check-Ins

- **Purpose:** To intentionally strengthen your joy-filled relationships.
- **How-To:** Identify three people who affirm your identity and joy. They might be friends, chosen family, or allies. Reach out this week to have a short, authentic check-in. It could be as simple as a text, phone call, or coffee meetup.
- **Alternative:** Plan a small gathering (virtual or in person) with people who affirm and celebrate your identity. This might be a themed movie night, a potluck, a game evening, or a casual hangout. Focus on creating an atmosphere where everyone feels seen and joy is the main goal. Afterward, reflect on what made the gathering joyful and what you might do next time.

TOOL: Affirmation Swap

- **Purpose**: To create a positive feedback loop that strengthens your friendship and reminds you both of your value.
- **How-To:** Reach out to a friend and exchange affirmations. Write each other a short note, message, or email highlighting what you admire about the other person and how they bring joy into your life.

TOOL: Queer Joy Journal

- **Purpose:** To notice the "glimmers" of queer joy all around you.
- **What is a glimmer?** A glimmer is something that reminds us that even in the midst of life's challenges, there's always a glimmer of joy. It's a small moment that can help us calm our central nervous system, relax, and feel happy, content, or joyful. A glimmer can be something as simple as petting a dog or seeing a rainbow. It's just a little something that reminds you that life is good and that there is beauty all around us.
- **How-To:** Keep a dedicated journal where you write down moments of queer joy that you experience each day. Over time, this journal can become a powerful reminder of how abundant joy can be, even during challenging times.

TOOL: Build Your Online Queer Community

- **Purpose:** To use the internet to connect with others who share your identity and values.
- **How-To:** Spend some time this week researching and joining one or two safe online spaces that feel welcoming. Start by exploring online platforms like queer-focused forums, social media groups, Discord servers, or virtual support meetups. Feel free to check out The Joyfully Queer Collective on Facebook to see if that may be a good fit for you!

This toolkit isn't complete without *your* voice. What relational practice brings *you* queer joy?

TOOL NAME: _____

Purpose: _____

How-To: _____

Conclusion

Feminist writer bell hooks once wrote: "When you wake up and find yourself living someplace where there is nobody you love and trust, no community, it is time to leave town—to pack up and go (you can even go tonight). And where you need to go is any place where there are arms that can hold you, that will not let you go.[1]"

In this section, we have talked about the importance of recognizing the community around us and building a chosen family that can hold us through both the good times and the hard times. I hope it has given you some hope that no matter who you are, where you live, and how you identify, there is a community out there for you!

Questions for Reflection:

- What does my ideal support system look like?
- Who do I count as family (both biological and chosen) and why?
- What role do allies play in my life, and how can they better support me?
- What queer media (TV shows, books, movies, music, etc.) helps me feel more connected to my community?

---

1. hooks, bell. *Sisters of the Yam: Black Women and Self-Recovery.* Boston: South End Press, 1993.

Mosaic Tile Four
Green–Nature

In the traditional Pride flag, the color green represents Nature. Belonging, growth, and being rooted are all essential in our journey of finding queer joy. For this mosaic tile, you are invited to reflect upon the following questions and then create a tile that represents the color green and the ways that queer joy helps you grow or feel rooted in your community.

Prompt:

- What grounds me when the world feels chaotic?
- How do queer friendships or relationships help me grow?
- What rituals or traditions have helped me feel at home?

Creative Exercise:

Use green to represent growth and belonging. Perhaps you paint vines, roots, or a forest clearing. Maybe it's a single sprouting seed. This tile symbolizes how your queer community helps you to thrive.

Example:

In this tile, I chose to create a mosaic within a mosaic, layering many shades of green together. Each distinct piece represents a different person, story, and lived experience within my community. The variations in green hold the richness of our diversity, yet together they form a single, living whole.

Section 4
Rooting Yourself in Liberation

"One of the most vital ways we sustain ourselves is by building communities of resistance, places where we know we are not alone."

— bell hooks, *Yearning: Race, Gender, and Cultural Politics*

In the spring of 2012, I joined 16 other young adults on the Soulforce Equality Ride. We rode together on a big, queer bus and traveled to Christian universities that had discriminatory policies against LGBTQ+ students. We also advocated for LGBTQ people in the communities we visited, and provided education and training about oppression, spiritual violence, and social justice.

We were a bunch of queer activists, but we never intended to be troublemakers on these campuses. Instead, our intention was to engage in dialogue with people who had been taught to use the Bible in ways that are spiritually abusive toward the LGBTQ community. Perhaps even more importantly, we wanted to show the queer students on these campuses, who were suffering in silence, that they were not alone. While they could not safely advocate for themselves, we could step in and be a voice for justice in their communities.

Each university we visited was chosen after students contacted us about their school's LGBTQ+ policies. The stories were heartbreaking. One former student shared with us that when he was suspected of being gay, he was attacked. Later, a teacher and three of his peers confronted him in a hallway, and gave him a surprise exorcism. When that did not save him from the "demon of homosexuality," he was expelled from the school and his records were sealed so he could not transfer his credits to another school. He was left with the loans from his expensive tuition and nothing to show for it.

Another student had been outed to her parents by her youth pastor, and they forced her into ex-gay therapy. She was attending a Christian university so she would be around "positive influences," and her parents had even shared her "same-sex attraction" with her advisor at school so her behavior could be monitored. She was battling depression and had attempted suicide twice since high school. She told me that she longed to find others who were like her in her community, but she didn't know how to do that safely. I was able to connect her with a local advocacy group in her area, and when I spoke to her two years later, she was living with joy because she had found a community that loved and supported her.

About halfway through our cross-country ride, we visited a college that would not allow us on campus. Not to be deterred, we held a peaceful demonstration on the public sidewalk. Several students came out to talk with us– both students who agreed with our message and students who did not.

Soon after our big queer bus pulled up, a young man with brown hair and bright eyes approached me and asked if I would be willing to talk to him. I said that I would love to, and we sat down together on the curb in front of the school. Connor told me that he wanted to talk because he believed the Bible was very clear that being gay was a sin and he couldn't see how anyone could interpret it differently. Unlike some of my other conversations while on the Ride, there was no hostility in his voice. He genuinely wanted to try to understand, even though it made him uncomfortable.

Over the next hour we prayed together, debated scripture, and shared stories from our lives. Little by little he let his guard down, and I saw a person who was passionate about both his faith and his love for others. He shared with me that as a member of the student government, he was a passionate supporter of his school. He also disagreed with the ways it discriminated against some of his classmates, and he didn't know how to reconcile that.

When the school locked down the campus to keep more students from coming out to meet with us, we decided to invite them to join us at a local coffee shop instead. Connor thanked me for talking with him and said he had to head to class. I gave him my contact information and invited him to reach out anytime if he wanted to continue our conversation. While it didn't seem like he had changed his mind about LGBTQ+ identities being sinful, I left hopeful that our talk had planted a seed that would prompt him to continue to ask questions.

Several students did join us at the coffee shop, and that afternoon we ended up having some of the most transformative conversations of our entire trip. One student emailed me to let me know that she was so angered by the way the college responded to us that she transferred to a different school the next semester. Another found me on Facebook afterwards to thank us for coming to her school. She said she was gay, but had never felt safe enough to come out to anyone before. She asked for resources to help her find a support system in her town, and I was able to connect her with an affirming community that supported her throughout the rest of her time there. I was hopeful that I would hear from Connor, but weeks turned into months and months turned into years. I was sure I would never see him again.

After the Equality Ride, I decided that if I wanted to continue to advocate for queer people in Christian spaces I should go to seminary. I moved to Kansas City and began earnestly studying the intersection between the Bible and queer identities. In my second year there, I was invited to attend a new conference for queer Christians with a group of my classmates.

During a social hour, I was holding a paper coffee cup in one hand and pouring sugar into it with the other when I felt a gentle tap on my shoulder. I turned around and saw… Connor? He was a little older and held himself with a lot more confidence, but it was him. "Excuse me," he said, "were you on the Equality Ride a few years ago?"

I was thrilled to see him again. We embraced and ducked out of the bustling hotel ballroom to find a quiet place to catch up. "What are you doing here?" I asked.

"That's… kind of a long story," he replied. Then, he proceeded to tell me about his life growing up as a conservative Christian. He had "struggled with same-sex attraction" since middle school, but refused to accept those feelings. He wanted to be a good Christian man, and he refused to give in to what he had been taught were sinful urges. And then, the Equality Ride came to town and changed his life.

"You were the first person I ever met who was both gay and Christian. I couldn't believe that anyone like you existed, and hearing about your faith was a shock to my entire system," he said. "After our talk, I began looking up every resource I could get my hands on about how to reconcile my faith and my sexuality. I went to therapy, I started working on accepting myself, and last year, I came out publicly."

My eyes welled up as I looked at him. He had the same brown hair and bright eyes that I remembered, but something about him was different. He was truly happy. Connor had discovered queer joy!

Community Action

Throughout this book, we have explored how queer joy is found in self-love and in community. I believe that we can maintain that joy by standing with that community through activism, advocacy, and mutual aid. When we organize to make positive change, we create joy that sustains us and points us toward a more just and hopeful tomorrow.

That joy can take many forms. Sometimes it looks like **resistance**, "pushing back against oppressive forces in the face of known risk.[1]" Resistance can mean anything from participating in boycotts and protests to making smaller, individual choices that fight back against oppression. For example, anytime a queer person chooses to embrace joy in a society that teaches us that being queer is a negative thing, they are resisting a harmful narrative about their own life.

Sometimes it looks like **resilience**, "the quality of being able to survive and thrive in the face of adversity.[2]" Resilience is the ability to stand back up and keep moving forward, even when we have been

---

1. Fakhoury, T. "Chapter 4 Eight Dimensions of Resistance." In *Pacifism, Politics, and Feminism*. Leiden, The Netherlands: Brill, 2019. https://doi.org/10.1163/9789004396722_006.
2. Meyer, I. H. "Prejudice, Social Stress, and Mental Health in Lesbian, Gay, and Bisexual Populations: Conceptual Issues and Research Evidence." *Psychological Bulletin* 129, no. 5 (2003): 674–697. https://doi.org/10.1037/0033-2909.129.5.674.

through trauma. Both resistance and resilience are essential to queer activism because they remind us that we need to tear down harmful systems while also caring for ourselves. Together, they are the heart and soul of collective action, ensuring that our fight for justice is infused with the joy of community and the hope of a brighter future.

Activism, advocacy, and mutual aid are three different methods of collective action that often work hand in hand. In the next few paragraphs, I will share examples from my time on the Equality Ride that show the different ways activism, advocacy, and mutual aid contributed to our work.

- **Activism** is a loud and visible call for justice. It can take the form of marches, rallies, protests, and collective action that disrupt the status quo and demand attention. On the Equality Ride, we did this by standing outside schools that refused to let us step foot on their property. By holding signs with messages about queer acceptance, chanting, singing, and speaking with passersby, we brought attention to the unjust ways these schools were treating their queer and trans students.
- **Advocacy** often happens in quieter, but equally powerful ways, like speaking with decision-makers, lobbying for policies, writing letters, or educating communities. For example, when schools allowed the Equality Riders on campus, we often met with faculty, staff, and board members. We were able to share with them the ways their policies were harmful, using real stories from their students. We also pointed them toward resources for creating safer schools and understanding the Bible in more affirming ways.
- **Mutual aid** happens when neighbors care for neighbors, communities pool resources, and we work together to make sure no one is left behind. While on the road, we were intentional about taking the time to volunteer at organizations in each city we visited. We sorted food at a queer food pantry, taught the basics of activism to queer youth at a youth center, visited with people living with AIDS at a group home, and joined with a queer-affirming church

to hand out lunch bags to unhoused persons in their neighborhood.

Activism stands up loudly and proudly for radical transformation, advocacy calls for systemic change, and mutual aid embodies the world we are fighting for by meeting immediate needs with empathy. These practices bring queer joy through the energy of collective resistance, the affirmation that our voices matter, and the love we show one another through compassion and care. When we stand together for justice, we are reminded that we create our own joy as we work toward a more equitable world.

Queer Activism and Advocacy

When most people think about joy, it's unlikely that megaphones, rallies, and speaking powerful truths in front of politicians immediately come to mind. However, activism and advocacy have always been sources of empowerment and joy for the LGBTQ+ community. Fighting for justice is not easy. It takes time, energy, and courage to stand up to unjust systems and policies. Just because something is hard does not mean it can't be joyful! Activism and advocacy can give us a sense of belonging and purpose, and bring us hope for the future.

The LGBTQ+ community has a rich history of standing up for justice and equality. As we discussed in the last section, Pride began as a protest and remains political to this day. During the AIDS crisis, ACT UP channeled grief into creativity, filling the streets with theater, chanting, and art, and refusing to let joy be extinguished. Ballroom culture has existed for decades as a form of activism and a sanctuary of joy for Black and Latinx queer and trans communities. According to the Human Rights Campaign:

> Aside from being a safe and welcoming space for many LGBTQ+ people, ballroom has also served as a bastion for community outreach, especially health-related outreach. Having been detrimentally impacted by the AIDS crisis during the 1980s and early 1990s, ball events came to serve as forums for

resourceful discussion around health, safety and prevention, galvanizing community members to take their health into their own hands. Today, ballroom events help connect folks to essential health and well-being information.[1]

Queer and trans folks continue to fight for justice and equity. In the summer of 2025, when rainbow crosswalks commemorating the victims of the Pulse Nightclub shooting were removed by the government, the community responded by re-drawing them with chalk or painting new ones in different areas of Orlando, FL. Organizations like The Trevor Project, PFLAG, and GLSEN work with school systems and city officials to create safer schools for queer kids. Wherever decisions are being made that affect our community, queer advocates can be found, doing the important work of educating and putting forward positive policies and legislation. No matter how challenging the fight, our community continues to come together and stand up for our rights.

This is not only important for creating positive change in society, it also creates positive change for us as individuals. Recent research on social movements has shown that activism and advocacy can foster positive emotions. In their study on the #MeToo Movement, Swanson and Szymanski found that "activism helped participants find their voice and regain their power. They described a process of moving from silence and shame around their sexual assault to freedom and empowerment.[2]" In another study on activism and positive psychology, Klar and Kassar found that collective action reduces feelings of isolation, strengthens resilience, and increases well-being[3].

For queer communities in particular, activism counters the shame and invisibility imposed by dominant culture with visibility, pride, and

---

1. Soto, J. "Honoring The History of Ballroom Culture During and Beyond Pride." *Human Rights Campaign*, June 28, 2024. https://www.hrc.org/news/honoring-the-history-of-ballroom-culture-during-and-beyond-pride.
2. Strauss Swanson, C., and D. M. Szymanski. "From Pain to Power: An Exploration of Activism, the #MeToo Movement, and Healing from Sexual Assault Trauma." *Journal of Counseling Psychology* 67, no. 6 (2020): 653–668. https://doi.org/10.1037/cou0000429.
3. Klar, M., and T. Kasser. "Some Benefits of Being an Activist: Measuring Activism and Its Role in Psychological Well-Being." *Political Psychology* 30, no. 5 (2009): 755–777. http://www.jstor.org/stable/41502458.

collective celebration. In a study on LGBTQ+ grassroots activism and resilience, researchers found that:

> …while minority stress was positively associated with poorer health, activism was positively associated with greater well-being. In other words, activism may enable LGBTQ+ individuals to positively respond to minority stress and economic precarity. Interestingly, the authors found even stronger associations between activism and well-being among youth of color than among their White peers. The authors suggested individuals most affected by minority stress experience the strongest effects of activism on well-being.[4]

When we face discrimination, prejudice, and hate, we need something to sustain us and help us keep moving forward. Activism and advocacy teach us to claim our own power in a system that wants us to be powerless. Standing up to oppression reminds us that we are in control of our own lives, and we are part of a strong community of queer folks and allies who will not be silenced. This empowerment is joy-filled, because we intentionally weave joy into our movements for justice.

Queer activism has always been especially creative, including sparkly drag queens in full regalia, glittery, often hilarious, signs with powerful messages, and lots and lots of rainbows. Marches are often full of protesters chanting, singing, and dancing… turning rallies into impromptu street festivals. These practices are declarations that our joy cannot be legislated away. Each time queer people bring humor, art, and beauty into public protest, we are building a future where we are free to live abundant and joyful lives!

---

4. Scheadler, T. R., K. R. Haus, T. A. Mobley, and K. P. Mark. "LGBTQ+ Grassroots Activism: An Opportunity for Resilience." *Journal of Homosexuality* 70, no. 9 (2022): 1675–1700. https://doi.org/10.1080/00918369.2022.2040928.

Mosaic Tile Five
Blue—Serenity

In the traditional Pride flag, the color blue represents Serenity. Finding peace is an essential part of finding queer joy! For this mosaic tile, you are invited to reflect on the following questions and then create a tile that represents the color blue and the ways that queer joy helps you find peace and serenity in your life.

Prompt:

- What gives me peace when the world feels heavy?
- How do I nourish myself while working for change?
- What kind of world am I dreaming of—and how can I help build it?

Creative Exercise:

With blue, express calm and clarity. Maybe it's a quiet ocean, a night sky, or a quilt of protest signs turned into stars. Let this tile be your reminder that rest is part of resistance, and that peace itself is a powerful form of joy.

Example:

In this tile, I chose to use a variety of blues to form gentle waves beneath a wide blue sky. The layered blues hold both movement and stillness, creating a sacred rhythm within it. The soft waves reflect the way my body and spirit need cyclical pauses to recover, breathe, and renew.

Mutual Aid

When my coaching client Xander first started attending his local trans support group, he wasn't going for himself. He was there to support his fiancée, who had just come out as a trans woman. As he sat back and listened, the group shared stories from their transitions. They talked about name changes and coming out, top surgery and hormones, voice coaches and new wardrobes.

Slowly, things started to shift for him. The stories he heard at the group didn't just impact him as an ally to the trans community, they resonated with something deep within him. He began to see parts of his own experiences reflected in the stories he heard. This group of kind strangers became his support system as he came to understand his own identity and transition himself.

When his relationship with his fiancé ended, he was left without housing. He could never have imagined how this community would step in to care for him. One person offered him a couch to sleep on, another brought him food, and others helped him raise the money to get back on his feet and find housing again. This group he had once tentatively attended to support someone else became his lifeline in the most challenging time in his life.

Years later, Xander still attends that same group. Now, though, he's the one welcoming new people to the circle. He remembers what it was like to be unsure, scared, struggling with coming out. So, he makes it a point to ensure that others feel the same kind of safety and acceptance that once saved him.

Xander has found joy in his community, and he does his best to spread that joy with the other people in his life. He cooks big batches of food for friends who are food insecure, meal preps for a friend living with a disability, and teaches others how to cook on a budget. He helps people sign up for food stamps. He knows that care isn't transactional, it's relational. It's what we do when we believe in each other's survival and joy.

In his town, Xander helps organize queer arts and crafts groups, donates to clothing swaps, and volunteers for a trans group where people are safe to show up as their true selves without judgment.

One of the beautiful things about the queer community is it makes room for you as you are, and it grows with you as you change. Xander began his journey identifying as a bisexual woman, then as nonbinary, and eventually found his truth as a trans man. Each shift came with new understanding, new language, and new relationships. "It's not just about being yourself," he told me. "It's about finding the words to name who you are and realizing that someone else has been there too."

Xander's story is a reminder that queer joy can be found in Pride parades and drag shows, but also in grocery runs, shared meals, affirming words, and clothes closets. This is the kind of joy that doesn't vanish in hard times. Rather, it's rooted in community, in care, and in mutual survival.

Mutual aid, community care, and collective care are all terms that describe ways in which a community comes together to provide for itself. Trans activist and author Dean Spade defines mutual aid as "... a form of political participation in which people take responsibility for caring for one another... not just through symbolic acts or putting pressure on their representatives in government but by actually building new social relations that are more survivable.[1]"

Mutual aid is most often found in the aftermath of a disaster or in

---

1. Spade, Dean. "Solidarity Not Charity: Mutual Aid for Mobilization and Survival." *Social Text* 38, no. 1 (March 1, 2020): 131–151. https://doi.org/10.1215/01642472-7971139.

marginalized communities who work together for survival. In the 1960s–1980s, the Black Panthers offered programs like "…the free breakfast program, the free ambulance program, free medical clinics, a program offering rides to elderly people doing errands, and a school aimed at providing a liberating and rigorous curriculum to children.[2]" During the AIDS crisis, it was queer networks that delivered meals, held bedside vigils, and created underground medical support. And during the COVID-19 pandemic, mutual aid groups organized online to provide rent assistance, mental health care, and safe housing to people in need.

Where I live, a mutual aid network has been created for the queer and trans community. Called the "Block Party," participants are invited to make new friends, share and learn new skills, and get help navigating local resources. There is always a meal, access to personal care and hygiene items, and a safe space to just spend time with other queer folks and allies. There is also usually someone from the community available to offer their services, from free haircuts to free legal advice. Others in the community teach things like proper bike maintenance or how to do arts and crafts. I have even led folks through the joy mosaic activity found in this book!

These bigger mutual aid networks are powerful and help numerous people, but mutual aid can also be found in individual situations. After the 2024 Presidential election, I was in a panic. My wife and I had had our son the month prior, and I knew that Donald Trump taking office again meant that my rights as a parent could be in jeopardy.

Despite spending thousands of dollars on sperm and reproductive healthcare and even being listed as the "father" on my son's birth certificate, I still had no legal protection as a parent. After hours of research, it became clear to me that the only way I could legally be his parent was through a second-parent adoption. The cost of sperm and fertility treatment, medical bills, hospital fees, and NICU care had depleted our savings, and we were struggling financially—there was simply no way I could afford to pay the $3500–5000 that local attorneys were charging for an adoption.

I felt defeated, depressed, and terrified. I felt as if I had no options left. And then, a friend of mine told me she was setting up a

---

2. Ibid.

GoFundMe to help raise money for the adoption. I was grateful, but still discouraged… It felt like there was no way that my small community could raise all the money I would need. Then, thankfully, I was connected with a queer lawyer who was doing discounted adoptions for queer couples before Trump's Inauguration.

Between the money that was raised through the GoFundMe, money that I saved from petsitting jobs, and a huge discount from the lawyer, I was able to adopt my son in December, 2024! Not acknowledging the legal rights of non-biological queer parents is one of the many ways that our community faces discrimination today. I am incredibly grateful that I had a community of care who helped me navigate these legal challenges and brought me the immense joy of legally becoming my child's parent.

From big groups working together to take care of a community to small acts of kindness that help one disenfranchised person get assistance, mutual aid networks are vital to the survival of queer and trans folks. These practices keep people alive, keep people healthy, build community, and yes—bring people joy. There is joy in seeing that we are not alone, joy in the relief of being cared for, joy in discovering that we have enough to share with others. Mutual aid turns despair into solidarity, and solidarity into celebration.

The Community Action Toolkit

As we've seen throughout this section, activism, advocacy, and mutual aid are important assets for our communities. When we are able to use our time and energy to work for justice and equity, it makes a huge difference! However, it can be challenging to figure out how to get involved for the first time. If you want to get started and don't know how, the first step is to find out where you can get involved locally, in your own neighborhood, local government, and networks of care. Getting involved doesn't require traveling to big cities or a full-time commitment to a cause. It starts with simply noticing what you are passionate about, what your community needs, and what networks are in place to meet those needs.

Howard Thurman has been quoted as saying, "Don't ask what the world needs. Ask what makes you come alive, and go do it. Because what the world needs is people who have come alive." In other words, there is so much injustice in the world that no one can realistically be involved with every single fight for justice. However, each person can choose one or two important causes and devote their passion, their energy, and their joy into making a difference there.

I care deeply about many causes, and over the past two decades I have volunteered or worked for a variety of social justice organizations. However, when I consider what I am most passionate about, I know that it is justice and equity for the LGBTQ+ community. Using this passion, I have worked with local and national organizations, traveled in a big queer bus around the country, and organized an LGBTQ+ wedding fair for queer couples in Kansas City.

In my work now, I give back to my community in several different ways. I do one-on-one coaching with folks who are trying to bring queer joy into their lives, I lead solo and group retreats, I teach classes and workshops about finding and embracing queer joy, and I speak and lead classes at churches, non-profits, and organizations that want to find joy in their work. I am hoping that through this book, my *Joyfully Queer* podcast, the Joyfully Queer Collective, and my individual speaking and teaching engagements, I will be able to continue spreading joy through our community.

There are many ways to fight for justice and equity for queer folks. I personally have chosen to focus on queer joy because I believe that it challenges the belief that queer lives are defined only by struggle or suffering. Without joy, movements burn out. Without joy, liberation is reduced to simply surviving rather than thriving. By cultivating joy, we remind ourselves and the world that queer life is worth defending **and** worth celebrating.

This is my passion. It is time to consider, what are you most passionate about? How do you want to make a difference in your community?

Are you passionate about reproductive healthcare? Try volunteering with a local reproductive justice organization, Planned Parenthood, or raising money for a national abortion fund. You could also write compassionate postcards or letters to people who have to travel for reproductive healthcare, or donate personal care items to abortion clinics and organizations.

Is racial justice your passion? You could organize a training on white privilege in your city or community center, stand up against racist language and behaviors in your own community, and volunteer for organizations like NAACP, Race Forward, and the ACLU.

Want to make sure unhoused and underprivileged communities have access to food and basic essentials? Try hosting a food drive, volunteering at a local homeless shelter, or food bank, or making up bags of shelf-stable foods and essentials to give away to people in need.

Is it hard for you to volunteer or organize in person? Try writing and sharing petitions, fundraising online, creating fliers for local events in your area, or contacting your representatives through postcards, emails, and phone calls!

Want to find joy through activism, advocacy, and mutual aid? Here are a few tools that you can try on your own:

TOOL: Show Up Locally

- **Purpose:** Building solidarity and visibility by joining with others in public spaces.
- **How To:** Find and attend a local gathering like a Pride event, a school board meeting, or a community march. Notice how it feels to be part of something bigger than yourself.

TOOL: Raise Your Voice

- **Purpose:** Speaking truth to power in ways that create change.
- **How To:** Write a short note or make a phone call to someone in power about an issue that matters to you. Share your story and why it matters personally.

TOOL: Answer the Call

- **Purpose:** Strengthening community through acts of care and generosity.
- **How To:** Respond to a mutual aid request from someone in your community. This could look like buying or making a meal, giving someone a ride, donating money, or picking up a bag of groceries.

TOOL: Share Your Time

- **Purpose:** Supporting movements and organizations that nurture queer joy and justice.

- **How To:** Give an hour of your time to a local queer group or community project. Even a small commitment can ripple out in powerful ways.

TOOL: Care for Your Circle

- **Purpose:** Practicing everyday solidarity and kindness.
- **How To:** Check in on friends and neighbors, especially those who may be isolated. A simple text, call, or visit can mean more than you realize.

This toolkit isn't complete without *your* voice. What practice brings *you* community action-based queer joy?

TOOL NAME: _____

Purpose: _____

How-To: _____

Conclusion

In this section, we've explored how activism, advocacy, and mutual aid can make the world a little safer—for ourselves and for our communities. Each week, my local "Block Party" sends out an invitation that carries this reminder: *We take care of us.*

I invite you to hold on to that truth. We take care of each other, and in that care, we find survival, resilience, and joy. As you give of your time, energy, and passion, don't forget to hold onto the joy that comes from giving back to our community!

Questions for Reflection:

- What issues stir my heart the most?
- Do I feel most alive when I'm marching in the streets, speaking up in a meeting, or quietly helping someone meet their daily needs?
- When was the last time I showed up for someone else? What kind of joy did that bring me?

Mosaic Tile Six
Purple–Spirit

In the traditional Pride flag, the color purple represents Spirit. Following your purpose is an essential part of finding queer joy! For this mosaic tile, you are invited to reflect on the following questions and then create a tile that represents the color purple and the ways that queer joy helps you find your purpose and legacy.

Prompt:

- What drives me to make a difference?
- How does my queer identity inform my values or advocacy?
- What legacy do I hope to leave behind?

Creative Exercise:

Let purple carry the depth of your spirit. Maybe it's a phoenix, a bridge, or a candle passed from hand to hand. This tile honors your commitment to justice, to future generations, and to joy as resistance.

Example:

In this tile, I chose to represent Spirit through a purple candle. The light shines in remembrance that queer joy is not only something we experience in the present, it is something we inherit and something we pass on. Each act of joy, tenderness, and truth becomes part of a living legacy, a flame that continues to be lit long after we ignited it.

Assembling Your Mosaic

Now that you've created all six tiles, take a moment to lay them out. You might arrange them in a single row, a circle, or in two rows of three. However you display them, let the final mosaic remind you:

- You are whole, even in your pieces.
- Your joy is real, powerful, and worthy of celebration.
- You are connected—to yourself, to others, and to a lineage of queer people creating beauty and meaning in a complex world.

Display your Mosaic of Queer Joy somewhere you'll see it often. Let it be your reminder to keep choosing joy!

Example Queer Joy Mosaic, Bethany Meier-Evans

Conclusion

"I want people to fall in love with themselves and to be really proud and full of joy for the space they take up. If someone else appreciates the space you take up, then that's icing on the cake."

— Jonathan Van Ness

I first started daydreaming about writing this book while I was on my honeymoon in Mexico. My wife, Kelsee, and I got married in October 2021, and a week later we were on our way to an all-inclusive week at a resort in Tulum.

Kelsee and I wanted to experience our honeymoon without having to wonder if the resort or its guests would be unfriendly to a queer couple. We didn't want to deal with awkward stares if we held hands or shared affectionate moments. We wanted to take romantic photos on the beach, have candlelit dinners, and simply enjoy our time together, free from worry that someone might say something ignorant or make us feel uncomfortable during such a special occasion.

While we normally would have planned our travel for ourselves, we decided to book through a lesbian travel company that would rent out the entire resort instead. They offered a jam-packed schedule of activities from dances to cooking classes to parties in the pool. We didn't participate in many of these since it was our honeymoon. But one moment stood out vividly for me.

I was sitting in our suite with the balcony door open when laughter echoed in from outside. Curious, I stepped onto the balcony to look. What I saw below took my breath away.

The resort was full of queer folks—mostly women, non-binary people, and trans folks—simply living their lives, fully and authentically. They weren't holding back, weren't toning down their queerness for the outside world. It was pure freedom. They knew they were in a safe place, surrounded by safe people. There was no need to second-guess whether they would be accepted, no fear of judgment or hostility.

As I stood there, I realized how important this kind of space is for our community. So many of us carry that little voice in the back of our minds, constantly questioning: *Is it okay if I kiss my partner in this pool? Will anyone have a problem if we hold hands while walking down the beach?* For many queer people, stepping into a public space that isn't specifically for a queer event (like a drag show or a Pride parade) means staying on high alert. It's that quiet but persistent voice asking, *Am I safe right now?*

But in that moment at the resort, none of those worries existed. I felt completely safe, and when I looked out at everyone around me, I saw nothing but pure, unfiltered joy. Throughout the week, I witnessed that same feeling again and again. The resort was full of queer people who were enjoying time with their partners, their friends, and making new connections without fear or hesitation. No one was self-censoring. No one was scanning the room before mentioning their significant other. They were simply there… fully present, fully themselves.

It struck me how much joy exists within our community, and yet how often that joy is overshadowed by narratives centered on struggle. Yes, challenges exist, but so does this immense, radiant happiness. That week in Tulum was a beautiful reminder of the power of queer joy, of the magic that happens when we have the space to *just be.*

This book is a product of that joy. My hope is that while we have been exploring what queer joy means and how we can invite more of it into our lives, we have also begun to shift the narrative that being queer is a burden. Andrea Gibson once wrote, "A difficult life is not less worth living than a gentle one. Joy is simply easier to carry than sorrow.[1]" We have been carrying the weight of our pain for so long, maybe it is time to pack lighter.

In this book, we have focused on three strategies that have been designed to help us to let go of some of our pain and embrace our joy.

In **Section One**, we discussed many of the burdens that we carry as queer people– minority stress, internalized queerphobia, discrimination, stigma, and institutional oppression. All of these stressors are a normal part of the queer experience, but they do not get to define who we are. We can choose to release the burdens that do not serve us and direct our energy towards creating and amplifying our joy.

In **Section Two**, we focused on the internal things we can do to bring more joy into our lives. The joy journey begins with learning how to love ourselves. Each of us is worthy of taking up space and experiencing love. When we believe that, we can start to build up our self-esteem, self-compassion, and self-acceptance. We can choose to ignore the mean, nasty voice of our Joy-Thief and listen to our Joy-Keeper instead. Through therapy, coaching, and self-love exercises we can find the source of our internal joy.

The joy journey continued in **Section Three** with external sources of joy like embracing and being embraced by our community. Our safe, affirming family members and chosen family are incredible sources of

---

1. Andrea Gibson, *every time i ever said i want to die*, [poem]

joy because they love us for who we truly are. Spending time with other queer folks in safe spaces, at community events, and during Pride, help us to feel more comfortable in our own skin. Our community helps us to know that we are not alone, that we are lovable as we are, and that our identity as a queer person is something to celebrate!

Once we have learned how to find joy through embracing self-love and love for others, we can channel some of that joy into giving back to our community. In **Section Four,** we focused on the power each one of us has to make the world a better place, whether we do that through sharing a meal with friends or protesting an unjust policy on the steps of the U.S. Capitol building. We have the power to dream big and to help make those dreams a reality through mutual aid, activism, and advocacy!

Thank you for joining me on this journey of finding queer joy. While we are reaching the final pages, I hope that you see this as a beginning rather than an ending. I invite you to carry forward the stories, practices, and reflections that spoke to your heart. Let them be reminders that joy is not something we stumble into by accident, but something we nurture with intention. Let them be a doorway into finding your own joy and inviting others to do the same.

This book is my love letter to queer and trans people everywhere. Never forget that you are beautiful, brave, and strong. Your worth is not determined by the bigotry of others or by shame from not-conforming to the status quo. You deserve to release societal expectations and live the life that is meant for you. You deserve love and joy **just because you exist** as your bright, shiny, incredible self!

If you want to continue on this joyful path, I would love to partner with you through my work with the Joyfully Queer Collective. Whether you want to join the Collective on social media and Patreon, attend my monthly classes or yearly retreats, do one-on-one coaching, or bring me into your organization for a workshop, sermon, or keynote, I would love to continue to be a part of your journey.

As we close, this is my wish for you:

> May you always remember that queer lives are full of joy, celebration, and connection.
> May you find joy in your body, in your spirit, and in your mind.
> May you create joy within your relationships, your community, and your chosen family.
> May you use joy to fuel you as you make this world a better place.
> May you continue to grow, to love, and to embrace your joy.
> And when you forget to be joyful—because we all forget sometimes—may you use the tools in this book to remind you how to embrace it once again.
> May it be so, today and every day.

The end.

www.ingramcontent.com/pod-product-compliance
Lightning Source LLC
LaVergne TN
LVHW050140080526
838202LV00062B/6540